THE TEAM LEADER'S HANDBOOK

How to help Christians serve Jesus **together**

DAVE MOORE

matthiasmedia
SYDNEY · YOUNGSTOWN

I first read Dave's material on team leadership as I stepped into a team-leading role in kids' ministry, and it gave me clarity and confidence as I approached this new way of serving Jesus. *The Team Leader's Handbook* will help you see the gospel heart behind team leading, before stepping you through the role and equipping you with a range of practical tools. It's simple, clear, really applicable, and biblically rooted in the desire to see Jesus glorified through ministry.

Sophia Lee
Kids Church Team Leader, Hunter Bible Church, NSW

There are so many leadership books out there, so why add *The Team Leader's Handbook* to your must-read list? Because Dave Moore is passionate about seeing your church raise up and deploy sacrificial, joy-filled team leaders who love to serve Jesus. Dave breaks down the job of building and deploying volunteer leaders in such a way that every leader in your church can easily grasp his framework and tools. And those leaders will then go on to equip even more leaders.

Steve Covetz
Lead Pastor, The Point Community Church, NSW

What a fantastic resource! I can't wait to get this into the hands of my team leaders. Dave Moore's book has given me a bunch of really clear, practical, principle-driven tools for effectively and lovingly leading a team. I love the focus on prayer, and the way Dave really pushes his readers to think realistically about how to put these tools into action week by week. I have a feeling a stack of these books will find their way into our church library and be a well-used resource for years to come.

Claire Williams
Pastor for Magnification, City on a Hill, Wellington, New Zealand

I'm so excited that this book has been written! Dave Moore shares wisdom gained from the successes and failures of years spent in building teams and encouraging and equipping team leaders. This book is accessible, theologically principled and practical—the four conversations tool is a winner! Put this in the hands of your team leaders (or potential team leaders) and use it as the basis for training.

Caroline Litchfield
Membership Director, Christ Church St Ives, NSW

Leading a team in church is an exciting responsibility, but it can also be very daunting! Dave Moore has written *the* book to dispel any fears and bring clarity to the task. Easy to read, warm, principled and thorough, *The Team Leader's Handbook* will help guide the new and long-term team leader in their noble task.

Dan Ford
Assistant Pastor, EV Church, Erina, NSW

I wish I'd had this book years earlier in raising up and equipping leaders who can empower and train future leaders. Dave Moore breaks down the gospel motivation and practical steps involved in leadership and insightfully addresses the particulars of leading volunteers. He has an obvious love for people and an enthusiasm for thinking deeply and systematically about how to lead teams well to bring glory to our Lord Jesus.

Jess Sheely
Assistant Pastor, Scots Church Sydney, NSW

I've had the privilege of working under and alongside Dave Moore for over ten years. He is a man who loves Jesus and has a wonderful desire for God to be glorified, for God's people to be loved, and for the lost to be saved. His evangelism and boldness personally helped me become a Christian, so I can't say anything bad about him. Nothing in this book is just theoretical for him; these are things he lives, breathes and puts into practice. He has a knack for knowing people and helping people learn.

I love this book because it's made for the volunteer team leader. So many leadership books have great ideas when you're working with people full-time, but they can be hard to implement in the context of the local church. This book started with seeing a great need to help churches equip our volunteer leaders for the sake of God's kingdom, and it has stuck to that purpose.

Scott Curtis
Pastoral Team, Hunter Bible Church, NSW

This book is a must-read for anyone in Christian leadership. For new leaders and established leaders alike, there are nuggets of leadership gold throughout. David Moore puts flesh on the bones of what it means for us to serve as part of Christ's body. He moves from principles to actions and shares insights from lived experience, all grounded in God's word. I'm excited to see the fruit of these principles within my own leaders and to see them grow in their godliness and faithfulness through serving our King.

Ling Shooter
Serving Minister, St Thomas' North Sydney, NSW

It might be easy to just do a task or delegate a task, but teaching and helping others think through the principles of *why* the task gets done is super helpful. In *The Team Leader's Handbook*, Dave Moore gives clear and concise guidance on moving from theory to practice, giving real-life examples of issues that arise when stepping up to lead ministry teams. It is so helpful, and so practical. It will help new and experienced team leaders alike to grow in self-awareness and deepen their love for their team members to see the joy in serving Jesus together.

James Hoey
MTS Director of Partnerships

Dave Moore starts with the Bible, helping us see how God uses teams of people for effective gospel ministry. From that platform, Dave offers a thorough application of how team leaders can lead gospel-centred teams. *The Team Leader's Handbook* provides a complete set of resources, alongside helpful real-life examples, that provide every team leader with the tools to lead their team effectively. Wonderfully, this book seeks to multiply the gospel by equipping team leaders to grow new leaders too.

Clare Merkel
MTW-MTS Partnership Developer

This is the best book I've read on leading ministry teams. The balance between biblical principles, practical skills and clear application is just right. I'd recommend it to anyone who is looking to grow as a godly, faithful and wise team leader.

Nathan Xing
Student Minister, Hope Anglican Church, NSW

The Team Leader's Handbook clearly lays out the distinct role of a team leader and how to put the principles of team leadership into practice. It's easy to read, and includes a bunch of really useful tools. I can't wait to read it with our current and potential team leaders.

Amy Stopher
Serve Purpose Leader, Providence Church, WA

Dave Moore has done us a great service in writing this book for pastors and Christian leaders. He has distilled years of thought and practical experience into a book that gives wonderful insights into many of the frustrations and joys leaders experience in the unique environment of the body of Christ.

Sam Hilton
City Campus Director, Hunter Bible Church, NSW

The Team Leader's Handbook
© Dave Moore 2024

Matthias Media
(St Matthias Press Ltd ACN 067 558 365)
Email: info@matthiasmedia.com.au
Internet: matthiasmedia.com.au
Please visit our website for current postal and telephone contact information.

Matthias Media (USA)
Email: sales@matthiasmedia.com
Internet: matthiasmedia.com
Please visit our website for current postal and telephone contact information.

Scripture quotations are the author's own translation.

ISBN 978 1 922980 33 5

Cover design and typesetting by Lankshear Design.

CONTENTS

To Jacob
Love, Dad

Sickle and plough, tractors and horses.
All hands! For the harvest is plentiful.

PART 1

TEAM LEADING MATTERS

1
—

SO, YOU'RE A TEAM LEADER

Let me introduce you to Steve

You probably haven't met Steve, but if you're involved in leading a team at your church, you might be feeling some of his pain.

Steve was a faithful, servant-hearted member of our church. He had been serving as one of the leaders at Kids Church (our Sunday morning children's ministry) for the past 18 months, and he was doing a great job. The kids and parents all loved him, and he had a great way of teaching the Bible to whatever age group he was leading.

As the year was coming to an end, we could see that our Kids Church leaders needed some support—they weren't really working together with a sense of unity. We decided they needed a team leader, and I thought Steve would be perfect. So, before the new year started, I sat down with Steve to have a chat about a potential new ministry role: the Kids Church team leader. It meant overseeing eight leaders and about 25 children each week. Steve seemed pretty excited. He was pumped about giving Bible talks to the kids, getting them doing craft and memory verses, and making it fun for everyone. He said yes, and dived straight into the role.

But after a few weeks, it was clear that Steve was wearing himself out. He was feeling stressed and over-burdened. We sat down to chat about it, and I asked him about the crew of people who were helping each week.

"That's just it", he said. "Not only do I have to plan out the kids' program and get that sorted; I also have to organize the team and tell them things to do.

Sometimes I think it would be easier if there were fewer people to lead!"

In that moment, Steve articulated just one of the many challenges that come with becoming a team leader. He was still trying to be *in* the team, while also being *in charge of* the team. He thought 'team leading' would be in addition to the role he was already doing, rather than seeing it as a completely new and different role. Essentially, Steve needed to rethink what it really means to be a team leader.

This might be something you need to rethink, especially if you're a volunteer leading volunteers.[1]

That's why I've written *The Team Leader's Handbook*.

I'm assuming you're reading this book because someone's asked you to lead some *thing* at your church. It might be a one-off *thing* or a regular *thing*. You might be brand new in the role, or you might have been leading this *thing* for a while. But this book is not about leading a *thing* for Jesus' sake. This book is about leading a *team of people* for Jesus' sake. After all, you can't really lead a *thing*, can you? You lead *people*. A group of people. A team.

Think about that for a second. The primary responsibility of a team leader is *not* to run the program; it's to run the team. The team members run the program, while the team leader runs the team.

Let me say that again; team *members* run the program, but team *leaders* run the team. This is the first really big idea I want you to grasp. Being a team leader is very different from being a team member.[2]

But it might be that you've picked up this book and you're not a team leader. Maybe you're a team member, or maybe you're leading other team leaders. Wherever you're coming from, it's worth understanding some of the key differences between being a team *member* and being a team *leader*.

---

1   I admit 'volunteers' is a strange word to describe those who have been "bought with a price" (1 Cor 6:20) and now joyfully count themselves as 'servants' of Christ (see 1 Tim 4:6). But I hope you'll bear with me in using it to describe the dynamics of leading a team of *unpaid* gospel workers (the focus of this book) as opposed to leading a team of *paid* gospel workers. In saying that, many of the principles I'll outline could still be relevant to the leader of a paid staff team.

2   Just to be clear; a Bible study leader is (generally) not a team leader. While they might have to do some aspects of team leading in the group, the role of a Bible study leader is similar to a kids' church leader: they are doing ministry *to a group of people*. But team leaders don't do ministry to a group of people. Rather, they help their team members do ministry *to a group of people*. Team leaders work *through* a team to serve other people. A Bible study leader is the front line, serving people directly.

Team leaders are different from team members

How is a team leader's role different from that of a team member? A helpful illustration might be the difference between a soccer player and a soccer coach: they both have the word 'soccer' in them, and they're both focused on succeeding at the same game, but they are very different roles, and they require different skills and different convictions. You can't just take a great soccer player and expect him or her to be a great soccer coach too.[3] In fact, *great players rarely make great coaches*.

It makes sense when you think about it. Great players love winning by being *on the field*. But great coaches love winning by being *off the field*—they love winning through their players.

Just imagine a soccer game where the players are all out on the field doing their thing, then one of the coaches suddenly jumps up from the sideline, runs onto the field, steals the ball from the opposition, and kicks a goal. That would be insane, right? Coaches are meant to stay on the sidelines and win the game *through their players*, not instead of their players, and not even alongside their players. The best coaches do their hard work off the field, to help their players win on the field.

That's the mindset every ministry team leader needs: they are trying to get their ministry done through their team members. Whether you're leading a Sunday setup team, or a weekend away team, or a holiday program team, or a staff team: leading the team doesn't mean *you* do the ministry; it means you lead *them* and empower *them* to do the ministry.[4]

I started talking with Steve about the difference between being a coach and being a player—how he had to start being the 'coach' for the Kids Church team. He had to cultivate a love of seeing his team members do the ministry. He had to find new joy in loving the kids *through* his team.

As we chatted, Steve seemed to grasp what I was saying. But then he paused

---

3   Football, I admit, would be the more appropriate term.

4   Does that mean a team leader never joins their team in the ministry? Isn't there a place for the player-coach? While the answer is 'yes' (as I'll discuss in chapter 16), I think this happens far more than it should. Team leaders usually stay in the team because they haven't worked out how (or why) to work *through* their team.

as though something had just sunk in. He looked a bit forlorn and said, "Does that mean I'll be doing less face-to-face ministry with the kids? What about the things that *I like* doing?"

I looked him in the eye and said, "Yes, that's what being a coach means, and it's what being a team leader means. You lead other people to do the ministry. You empower other people to do the things you love doing. In fact, it means you start to prefer it. You choose to enjoy stepping back, rather than stepping in. I know that sounds a bit confronting now, but trust me, it's great!"

Do you see how being a team leader is very different from being a team member? It's not a subtle difference. Why? Because it's not just a different set of tasks; it's a different way of viewing yourself. There's a real change in self-perception that new team leaders in church and ministry organizations must wrestle with. There are real pain points people feel as they step into leading others. Both in my own experience of leading teams, and as I've trained team leaders over the years, learning to lead others almost always involves some internal challenges, perhaps even some grief.

Let me share three of the most common challenges you might face as you make this shift.

Challenge 1: Changing your 'ministry time'

In a world that's made a god of being busy, people have become very aware of where they spend their time. So it's common for Christians to think about the time they serve while at church as the time they're serving Jesus. That is, many Christians who are involved in some ministry in their church only have a limited amount of time in their week to devote to that ministry. For the most part, it's when they are directly involved in the ministry *thing*. For example, if Tom is a member of the Youth team, most of his time doing youth ministry is on Friday nights, 6–9 pm. He might do a little bit of prep during the week, but generally speaking Tom considers his 'ministry time' as the time spent 'doing things *with* youth' at youth group.

But if Tom were to become the Youth *team leader*, that will dramatically change when he spends his 'ministry time'. As the team leader, Tom's focus is helping his team members prepare for Fridays. And you can't prepare for Friday while Friday is happening. Tom needs to do things like calling his leaders, making sure they know their responsibilities for next week, and ensuring someone is contacting the new kids. Tom's main ministry time is *not* Friday night. In fact, when it comes to Friday night, in an ideal world, Tom just steps back and watches as his team goes about doing the things he's already arranged. In fact, he'll spend Friday night watching and working out what conversations he needs to have with his team members *after* the event in preparation for next week.

Consider how a soccer coach spends all week preparing his team, then watches the game from the sidelines. During the game, the coach can only offer little bits of feedback here and there. He has very little control over the course of the game while it's on. But once the game is over, it's the coach's time to shine. While he's watching the game, a good coach is thinking, "Okay, this week we're going to need to work on passing, and I need to have a private conversation with Sonya about her attitude ..."

If you're going to be a team leader, it's important to come to terms with the idea that team leaders do the bulk of their ministry *in between events*, not at events. At the event, you oversee your team do their thing. In between events, you're helping them prepare for the next event.

Challenge 2: Changing relationships

There's no getting around the reality that being a team leader will affect your relationships with your team members. While you're relating to them in this role, you have some authority over them. That might be a very new or strange dynamic to bring into an existing relationship. They might be your friends, or they might be older than you or have been Christians longer than you. But now, in the context of this ministry team, you're their 'team leader'. And let's be honest: some people find this awkward.

Whether you want that authority or not, being a team leader means you have the ability to do things like:

- invite new people into your team
- set a team's culture and values
- give people new roles and responsibilities
- change the team's future plans
- ask people to leave your team.

These are not insignificant powers, and many of your team members will start to see you in light of these powers (regardless of whether you've even used them). People might start to treat you with a different attitude—a new sense of caution, or respect, or even disdain.

As we become aware of these changing relational dynamics, a potential mistake is to treat our team-member relationships as equivalent to a secular employer-employee relationship. While many Christians have team-leader roles in their workplaces, they often find it difficult to lead their ministry teams like they lead their work teams. There are several reasons for this, but two key differences are that the basis of your relationship is very different, and the basis for their decision to be a member is very different. In a ministry context, your team members are eternal brothers and sisters in Christ, and they're (hopefully!) motivated by love, not by money.

But despite those important differences, it's important to be aware that becoming a team leader adds an extra dimension to your existing relationships with the members of your team.

⬧

After Steve and I last spoke, he started trying to lean into his role as the guy who leads the kids' team, not the guy who does the kids' ministry. We caught up a week or so later to see how it was going.

"It just feels really strange", Steve said. "Some of these people on my team have been close friends for years. I used to flat with Pete, so it feels weird being his 'boss' on Sunday afternoons. Then there's Renee, who's been a primary-school teacher her whole life. I've learned more from her over the past few weeks than anyone. It just feels wrong that I'm the team leader."

"Yeah, I get that", I said. "There's a new layer to your relationship with all these people. You're Pete's mate *and* you're his Sunday Arvo Kids Team Leader. It's not one or the other. But it is a new aspect of your relationship. Same with Renee—your relationship with her is kinda like a master with a student, where you're the student." Steve nodded emphatically.

"But it can be multilayered", I continued. "You can be her student *and* be her team leader at the same time. Being the team leader doesn't mean you know everything or that you're the expert in the room. Remember, the soccer coach is not the best soccer player in the team. He's responsible to make sure every player on the team has the greatest impact."

"So I can be their friend *and* learn from them *and* be their team leader—all at the same time? That feels like I'm wearing lots of hats all at once. What if I make a decision or do something they think is wrong or unwise?"

"Well, if that happened, what would you hope they would do?" I reflected back.

"Well, I'd like them to speak up and tell me what they think would be better", he replied.

"Totally. So that means part of your job as the team leader is to cultivate a team culture where everyone feels comfortable letting you know if there's a better way to do things. As the team leader, you play a big role in setting that dynamic."

Just like in Steve's experience, being a team leader brings a new layer to the relationships you have with your team members. It's totally possible to be someone's friend *and* be their team leader at the same time. In fact, this should be a strength in Christian relationships because it's how Jesus relates to us: he's our Lord *and* he's our brother. But we'll look at that more soon.

This is also challenging because leading people often means asking them to do things they don't want to do. And these people are usually volunteers, right? As I mentioned earlier, you can't just tell them what to do in quite the same way that you might with employees at work. The usual management skills and techniques that *might* work in the secular workplace won't always fly in the volunteer world.[5] How do you tell a friend that they need to do something again because they didn't do it right the first time? How do you maintain a close relationship while dishing out instructions and feedback, and generally telling people where you want the team to go?

I don't want to downplay this challenge. There's a good chance that you will have either experienced or witnessed a broken relationship in church life because of how a team member treated their leader or how a leader treated their team member. But I also want to offer hope and encouragement. There are some simple tools you can use as a team leader to help manage these team

---

5   I'd argue, however, that the techniques you use to lead people at church will always be applicable when leading employees outside church. Indeed, many modern secular leadership consultants and authors recommend a strong focus on understanding and working with an employee's passions and existing motivations, rather than leaning on top-down authority.

dynamics, and we'll go through those soon. On top of this, I've seen and been part of numerous teams that have lasted for years and have been a real place of joy while serving together. So, while there will always be times when Christian relationships are stretched (see Acts 15:36–41), we should prayerfully expect that Christians can and will work well together in ministry teams.

Challenge 3: Changing what you love about ministry

One of the biggest pain points of becoming a ministry team leader is how it changes what you love about ministry. Becoming a team leader usually means cultivating a newfound love for helping others do the ministry they love. One way of saying this is that you need to learn to love watching.

Sitting back and watching other people do the work seems like a terrible way to express leadership, but I don't mean this in a slacking-off, master-slave way. I mean finding real joy and pleasure in seeing your team come together, serve Jesus, and love other people really well. Think of a parent who spends years driving their child to piano lessons, then one day cries tears of joy as they watch their child perform on stage. That's the kind of joy I'm talking about: the joy of watching your team, people in whom you've invested time and prayer and energy, work together to grow Jesus' kingdom.

Much like the change in relationships, this is not an either/or thing. Just as team members don't stop being your friends, you don't stop loving the ministry you've been doing. And you certainly don't stop being motivated by the gospel to see Jesus' kingdom grow. Rather, leading others becomes a new expression of the same heart, a new kind of ministry to start loving, a new way to serve and glorify Jesus. So, keep your current love of serving Jesus, and ask him to help you cultivate a greater love for helping your team serve him.

This is a mind shift—or perhaps a *heart* shift—where the concern and love you already have for Jesus and his people drives you to focus on your team members in a new way. It's a decision to so love the people affected by your ministry (i.e. the children, in the example of Kids Church) that you serve the team who are responsible for loving them. It's loving people *through* your team for Jesus' sake.

I wish there was a simple way to flick this switch inside your heart. I wish you could read this section and say, "Oh, okay, so I just stop being *solely* motivated by my love of welcoming people at the door, and be *even more motivated* by a love of seeing my team members serve Jesus by welcoming people at the door. [Insert sound of internal cogs grinding—click.] Done!"

If only.

The reality is that this mind shift and heart shift probably won't happen quickly. But over time, this is the shift you need to make in your heart for your own sake, but more importantly for the sake of your team and for the sake of the gospel. Cultivate a love for serving Jesus in a new team-leader type of way.

So, there are our three aspects of being a team leader that may be a challenge for you:

1. A Christian team leader's 'ministry time' is usually focused outside the 'main event' (rather than during it).
2. A Christian team leader has a multifaceted relationship with their team members.
3. A Christian team leader cultivates a love for watching their teams do great things for Jesus.

There are more challenges we could discuss. But how do you face these challenges if you're just starting out?

Facing challenges with the gospel and tools

If you're reading this and feeling a bit swamped, please trust me—it's going to be okay. The good news is that as God's forgiven and Spirit-filled children, we have great hope when it comes to change. And we have great hope when it comes to working together for Jesus. We believe in a God who changes our hearts, develops our character, and uses different parts of his earthly body to work out his plans and purposes.

We also believe that God has given us a generally well-ordered world where we can use practical wisdom to help us do the things we want to do. There are various practices, methods and tools for leading teams that usually work most of the time. But even these pragmatic things can be gospel shaped; we can tweak them with gospel principles in mind.

In other words, the gospel of Jesus gives us a heart for how we lead teams, and it shapes the tools we use to lead those teams well.

That's essentially the outline for the rest of this book.

In the rest of part 1, we'll look at how the gospel shapes team leadership. In the following sections, we'll focus on what a Christian team leader does. Part 2 is about what team leaders *always* do; part 3 is about what team leaders *regularly* do; part 4 is about what team leaders *often* do. We'll spend the lion's share of the book in these later parts because my goal is to be very practical—for example, to provide a model for having conversations with your team, and to share tangible steps you can take and use in your ministry straight away.

Finally, in part 5, I'll take you through some other tools that will help you reflect on your team and where you might need to focus your time and energy once you get going.

At various points along the way, I'll share some real-life examples. Some names have been changed, and some conversations have been condensed (like the conversations with Steve I've already shared), but they're meant to paint a picture of how these ideas affect real people in real churches. I'll also give you opportunities to pause and reflect—either on your own, or with other people. And I'll suggest some prayers that you might like to pray.

This last point is very important. Leading a team of Christians for Christ's glory is a great privilege, but it's a task we can only fulfil with God's help. I hope you'll take these opportunities to ask God to help you absorb what you've read and become the type of leader he wants you to be.

In fact, let's start by praying a prayer together.

> Dear Father God,
> Thank you for Jesus, and for the absolute privilege it is to serve him and serve his people for his glory. As I find myself in the role of team leader, I don't just want to do a good job; I want to please you too. With that in mind, please help me to grow as a team leader. Please help me learn the lessons you want me to learn from this book, and help me to use what I learn to serve others. Amen.

Why I wrote this book

Remember when Steve told me, "Sometimes I think it would be easier if there were fewer people to lead"? That was an important moment for me too. In fact, if you're reading this and you're in vocational church leadership, it might be something you need to hear.

When Steve said those words, I realized I had made a mistake: I had assumed Steve would just work out how to change from being a *leader of kids* to being a *leader of a team* (that happens to lead kids). I thought Steve would automatically know what a team leader is meant to do, or he'd work it out for himself. It was a silly mistake to make, but it's also a very common mistake. It usually goes something like this:

1. A church leader like me will see someone like Steve, who is a great team member (e.g. a great children's leader, or a great welcomer, or a great setup person).
2. They assume that person will be a great team *leader* of people who do that thing.
3. They ask them to lead the team of people doing that thing.
4. They get frustrated when the newly appointed team leader reverts to doing the thing rather than leading the team to do the thing.

Essentially, people like me forget the enormous difference between being a member of a team and being a leader of a team. And that was my mistake. I shouldn't have simply appointed Steve to *be* a team leader; rather, I should have helped Steve *become* a team leader—for his sake, for his team's sake, and for Jesus' sake.

That's what this book is all about. This isn't just another book on Leadership. Yes, we'll look at the big principles of leading a team in your church or ministry context. And there will be practical examples and various action steps you can take straightaway. But my big prayer is that this book will help you embrace the wonderful ministry of leading Christians who are serving Jesus together.

Reflection questions

1. Have you ever had a great team leader (in church or secular environments)? What can you pinpoint about what made that person a great leader for you at the time?

2. Steve had to wrestle with the "change from being a *leader of kids* to being a *leader of a team*". Do you feel like you've had to go through that same kind of change? How have you found the change?

3. As you think about becoming a team leader, which of the three "pain points" do you feel most?

- Changing your view of 'ministry time'.
- Changing relationships with your team members.
- Changing what you enjoy doing.

4. What aspects of being a team leader are you hoping this book will help you with?

2

TEAMS ARE WORTH THE PAIN

At this point, you might be wondering if it's even worth being a team leader. It certainly sounds like a lot of hard work and personal pain. Why have ministry teams at all? Many churches have operated just fine for years without 'teams', right? What if all this work to be a team leader is just a fad that will get replaced by something new in a few years anyway?

As we begin thinking about these big questions, let's first make sure we're clear what we're talking about.

What do I mean by 'team'?

Throughout this book I'm going to refer to 'team ministry'. By this I mean *a group of Christians who collectively take responsibility for a gospel-motivated outcome within their church or ministry organization.*

Let me expand on this definition.

A group of Christians

A team is usually more than two or three people (depending on the outcome being sought). If you're trying to be the team leader of two people, it might create a weird dynamic. You'll almost certainly end up being a team player while also being a team coach. While this is certainly possible, I'm usually going to be referring to a team of three or more people. And I'm assuming they're all Christians because only Christians are indwelt by Jesus' Spirit and can therefore participate in his work (i.e. gospel work).

Collectively take responsibility

A team has a shared responsibility that is greater than the personal responsibilities of the individual members of the team. It is a group of people who are all committed to a common purpose—the team's purpose. For example, in Acts 6 a team of men were chosen for a set purpose (to free up the apostles by taking over the responsibility of distributing food to widows). In the same way, a church band has members who share responsibility for the whole song, which might mean they don't even play part of it. But not playing can be one of the ways they seek to fulfil the larger responsibility of serving others in song. The big idea is that all team members do their individual parts for the sake of an overall shared goal.

For a gospel-motivated outcome

A team is focused on a kingdom outcome, rather than simply performing a series of actions or running an event. For example, the band hopes to see people praise God, the setup team wants to ensure new people find their way easily into church to hear the gospel, the welcome team wants to help new people connect and join church well, and the team running the evangelistic course wants to see people become Christians. Therefore, these teams don't just *do tasks*; they're given a certain amount of responsibility (and therefore authority) to decide what tasks need to be done to best achieve their outcome, under God, for the sake of the gospel. They have an eye to the eternal results, not just the to-do list.

Within their church or ministry organization

The kind of team I'm describing is itself part of a larger church family. It is part of the body, playing its role for the sake of the whole church (see 1 Cor 12:7). It's not trying to go rogue or do its own thing. It comes under the authority of the larger church or organization, and it derives its purpose and responsibility from that. In other words, a team is neither self-appointed nor autonomous.

Rosters are not teams

Let me take this one step further to be as clear as possible; rostering people to help at church is not team ministry. Roster-based ministry and team-based ministry are very different things. Rosters, or rotas (depending on what part of the world you're from), are typically about assigning tasks to people rather than inviting them to think hard about the big outcome and take responsibility for it. This means they are less flexible and less equipped to handle urgent or unexpected issues that arise. Similarly, while rosters might bring a few people together for a common task, their ad-hoc nature means there's little coordination around how to best achieve the outcomes as a group; there's very little scope for reflecting, changing, using one another's gifts, or growing and developing as a whole.

Please don't hear me say that rosters are bad—far from it! My point is to try and delineate the difference between two models of Christian service. If you see yourself as a team leader because you coordinate a roster of volunteers, please don't read the rest of this book thinking that's what I'm talking about. It's an important way of serving the body of Christ, but it's not what I'm addressing. When I talk about 'team ministry', I'm referring to a group of Christians who—with God's help and with your leadership—have committed to serve *together* and who prayerfully feel a weight of responsibility for a shared goal.

I think there's something very Christian about serving together with this type of team mindset. In fact, I'm convinced that coordinating our ministry efforts through teams like this is an expression of how God has made us, how he saved us, and how he now uses us. Let me explain more of what I mean by turning to the Scriptures.

Created with teams in our blood

When you start thinking of a team as a group of people who have been appointed to work together for a gospel purpose, it does seem that God is very fond of teams. From the very beginning in Genesis 1–2, we see God literally create a team in Adam and Eve (and their children). God gives that team a purpose: to rule and bring good order (1:26–28). God gives them roles and responsibilities, such as naming the animals and working the ground (2:15, 19). The first family is what I'd call a *type* of team. It follows that every family is a shadow of that first team. A household is a kind of 'team' that is seeking to fulfil God's purposes together and in their various roles (if they are following God's design). Joshua speaks as a true team leader when he says, "as for me and my family, we will serve Yahweh" (Josh 24:15).

But apart from families, we see many other expressions of teams as we see God's people work together. As Jesus gathers followers, he gives them responsibility. For example, in Luke 10 Jesus sends the disciples out in pairs and entrusts them with a certain amount of authority. In Luke 8, the women with Jesus were part of his team as they helped provide for the needs of their Lord (vv 1–3). In Matthew 28, the disciples are given an outcome to strive towards: to make disciples of all nations (v 19). In Acts 1, they are given a goal of witnessing to Jerusalem, Judea, Samaria and the ends of the earth (v 8).

Looking at the picture of ministry in the New Testament, we find it is consistently performed by groups of people working together. As mentioned above, Acts 6 shows the apostles appointing a team of people to take responsibility for a pressing church need (vv 1–7). In Acts 13, the Holy Spirit appoints Paul *and* Barnabas to take the gospel to the Gentiles (vv 2–4), and they work with a team of "companions" to fulfil this task (v 13). Timothy and Titus are told to appoint not one leader, but multiple leaders, who are to take responsibility for the family of believers in each town (2 Tim 2:2; Titus 1:5). These 'oversight' teams in each church are made up of people who undertake different roles:

> Ensure the elders who govern well are given two-fold honour, particularly the elders who labour in the word and teaching. (1 Tim 5:17)

Notice the implication that while some elders are responsible for teaching, other elders—who don't teach—are still part of the same eldership team. One team, one purpose, but many roles within the team.

We see the same principle played out with Paul and Timothy. In Acts 16, Timothy joins Paul and Silas in their gospel work. In fact, it seems that proper gospel work is always inviting people in to be part of the ministry action (as Paul says in 2 Timothy 2:2).

In 1 Corinthians 12, Paul paints a picture of the church family as a sort of team, where everyone uses their own unique gifts and circumstances for the good of others. Just like a body, each member of the church has a role to play in the overall health of all the other parts. They all share a common goal of wanting to see one another grow in Christ. The point seems to be that all Christians— simply by virtue of being Christian—are called to be part of God's team and to work together in growing each other. Look at how Paul says this in Ephesians 4:

> Jesus gave ... shepherds and teachers to the holy people so they would be ready for the work of service, to build up Christ's body until we all become united in the faith and knowledge of God's son—completely mature in the fullness of Christ. (Eph 4:11–13)

Christian churches are like a big team—all called to participate with God in his work and his purpose. We're not just invited into the family; we're also invited into the family business of seeing one another grow to be mature in Christ.

Look at how Peter says this in 1 Peter 4:

> As each of you have received a gift, use it for the purpose of serving each other as good stewards of God's varied grace. (1 Pet 4:10)

Paul says a similar thing in 1 Corinthians 12:

> There are various outworkings, but the same God is working all things in everyone; to each is given an expression of the Spirit for the common good. (1 Cor 12:6–7)

As Christians, God calls us to work *with* his gifts *for* his ends *in* the lives of others. This should really astonish us: we get to be part of God's work! We get to be co-workers of God himself (as Paul calls himself and others; see 1 Cor 3:9). We're not only God's children; we're part of his crew, part of his team.

A note on roles and values

It's worth pausing here to reflect on how the world values people compared to how the church is called to value people.

There is a fear among some Christians that if we focus too much on people serving, we'll end up giving greater value to those who are up-front or seemingly successful, and we'll devalue people who might not be able to serve in those ways. This might be a legitimate fear, but only if we value people the way the world does.

We live in a world that wants to connect a person's value to their role or their success. The world around us looks for jobs and careers to make themselves feel valuable and to determine the value of others. But that is an evil way to view people, because it devalues those who don't do seemingly 'valuable' things. We have become a meritocratic culture where you must prove your worth (to yourself or others) through what you achieve.[6]

Yet the gospel turns this idea upside down. In the gospel, God adopts us—wicked and worthless people—in his Son, and gives us his Holy Spirit. We have imputed value, not based on the value of our work, but because of our union with Christ, the truly valuable one. Christians don't need to chase value in this life, because we've been declared valuable in the gospel.

This affects the way we see people's involvement in ministry. The spiritual reality is that a person's value is *not* determined by the work they do or the role they play. Rather, they are invited to work and serve in their own way *because* they already have gospel-given value.

This has massive implications for how Christians do team ministry. We shouldn't give people special treatment because they serve in valuable ways. If anything, we should look for ways to give special treatment to those who can't serve in those big, noticeable ways:

> God has assembled the body, giving more honour to the lacking,
> in order that there may not be division in the body, but that
> all the members may have the same concern for one another.
> (1 Cor 12:24–25)

Since the church family is a sort of team working together for the good of one another, everyone has their place, and nobody's value is determined by the value of their role. There is no place for pride or boasting in those who happen to have gifts that are more visible and prominent.

This principle should be applied to smaller teams that operate within the larger church family/team. People serving together in ministry teams are meant to value one another, not based on what each person 'brings to the team', but based on the gospel truth that we have been mercifully adopted as sons and

---

6   I think this is why our world has largely devalued the elderly, the institution of motherhood, and the unborn: they are considered less valuable because—in the world's eyes—they do not 'produce value'.

daughters (Rom 8:14-17; Gal 4:5-7) who now work in the family business together by grace alone (Eph 2:8-9).

Working together in God's image

This picture of God's adopted family working together in teams—where each person plays their role for a greater purpose—is fitting for people who have been created by the triune, relational God. The God who is Father, Son and Spirit works together as one, such that what the Father determines, the Son works through the person of the Spirit. It's team-like! In a sense, every human team is just a shadow of the God we worship and serve. When the tech team works together to support the band and the preaching of the word, they are playing out a dim shadow of the shared purpose and work of their triune God.

The point I'm making is that part of being made in God's image seems to be that he has made us as inter-dependent beings. We're designed to work together, to play different roles, and to give thanks for one another's existence and for one another's gifts and strengths. God uses his people to transform his people. He doesn't just zap us with the Holy Spirit and make us perfect copies of Jesus, but he does make us more and more like Jesus through the work of other people—through *teams* of other people! From the apostles who wrote the Scriptures to the crew that sets up the church for the people of God to gather around his word, God uses these teams of people as part of his big team to change you and me. As John Stott wrote:

> There is immense value in the team concept, as I know from experience as well as Scripture, because then we capitalize on one another's strengths and supplement one another's weaknesses.[7]

Teams seem like a pretty valuable way to gather and mobilize Jesus' church. And if that's what teams do, it makes the role of team leaders very important. As a team leader, you get the privilege of helping a small group of God's children focus on loving many others and growing his kingdom in a particular way. Christian team leaders help Christians better express what it means to be great members of God's big team.

7   JRW Stott, *I Believe in Preaching,* Hodder & Stoughton, 2014, p 107.

The practical value of teams

In addition to the theological realities, I'd also like to suggest that humanly speaking, people (and churches) just work better when they work together in teams. Teamwork very often leads to wonderful results. Here are just a few positive outcomes we can expect.

Teams become places of Christian fellowship

Christians often make lifelong friends by serving Jesus together on a team.

When people commit to being part of a team, they are not simply committing to doing a task 'at the same time'; they are committing *to one another* as team members. This means they come together and share the load and the responsibility with each other. They bear one another's burdens as they work together for a shared goal. This is often where Christian friendships are forged. Deep Christian fellowship is more likely borne in labouring together than lounging together.

Teams excite and empower people to improve things

Teams provide an avenue for people to take responsibility and make ministries better. Let me explain what I mean.

When we started running a Wednesday morning women's Bible study, we arranged a roster of people to run a crèche (childcare program) while the mums read the Bible together.[8] This crèche was working okay, but it was always a mad rush trying to fill the roster, and it wasn't always a great experience for the kids.

This went on for a few years until Andrew started running crèche. He could see it wasn't really working as a rostered job, so he decided to build a team. He recruited some people to make Wednesday morning crèche "their thing"— he gathered them together to talk about *why* they do it and what type of experience they would love the kids (and their mums) to have.

The team became so excited. They came up with a name for the ministry ('Lil' Buds' rather than just 'crèche'). They worked out a teaching program. They arranged new toys and a way of cycling through sets of toys to keep the kids from getting bored. They developed good ways of managing children who got upset or wanted their mum. The program became much better, all because

---

8   In Australia, 'crèche' refers to a childcare program for very young children.

Andrew invited people to see it not just as a task they are rostered on to do, but as a responsibility they cared about as a team. They still had to fill in some gaps with rostered helpers, but even those people had a better experience and a better attitude to serving, because they could see they were helping out on a team with a purpose.

Generally speaking, teams outperform rosters because teams can take responsibility for coming up with ideas, executing them, tweaking them, and improving them. And that generally means teams will end up doing a better job of loving people.

Teams are better at loving people

While outcomes aren't everything, we should care about them. We should want to love people well, and we should be prepared to ask ourselves whether we and our church are doing a good job of loving people. I'm convinced that in almost every ministry circumstance, teams are better than individuals at loving people.

Let me give you one example: how do you love newcomers? A church welcomes people not just by saying "hello", but by inviting them into the life and community of the church. You can leave this up to individuals to do in an ad-hoc fashion—imagine a new family arrives at church, and they sit next to dear old Deloris. You can *hope* she tells them about your church's values and key structures, and how you'd love them to be part of the family, and what that might look like for them. But the reality is that Deloris probably doesn't even realize they're new, let alone that there's a kids' program on Fridays for their 10-year-old son.

In other words, on her own Deloris probably won't do a great job of loving this new family *into the life of church*. She'll love them by being nice to them, and it will be totally 'authentic'. But it's not the type of love they need at that point. They need a special expression of love that is all about helping them work out if this is a church they're going to partner with in the coming years.

But now consider the alternative: you establish a team of people who lovingly and prayerfully coordinate welcoming, and who think about how to help different newcomers feel loved and informed about your church. That team can help Deloris (and the rest of the church) learn how to welcome people better, and can play a long-term role in walking with people as they join a new church (which usually takes 3–6 months).

Over time, a defined and organized welcoming team will always do a better job of loving people than just assuming that welcoming will 'happen authentically' as newcomers meet members of your church.[9] And the same dynamic will play out in most areas of church life.

Teams need team leaders

All in all, we can conclude that ministry teams provide Christians with fertile ground to express their gifts, love their church and the world around them, and grow in their gospel impact over time. But here's the catch: teams need team leaders.

Without a team leader, a team isn't really a team. Without a team leader, a team will always struggle to know where it's going and how it's doing.

Teams need people (like you) to lead them.

Teams need people to go through the pain of becoming a team leader, so that they can be better teams and love people better. Remember the three challenges that most new leaders face:

1. changing your 'ministry time'
2. changing relationships
3. changing what you love about ministry.

I hope you can see why going through these changes is worth it. If you believe that Christians work best in teams, then I hope you'll also believe it's worth going through some personal challenges to be a better team leader.

9   If your church doesn't have a team doing this and you think it is doing a great job of welcoming new-comers, that's great! But I'm going to guess it's probably due to a small group of individuals who do pretty much all the welcoming—almost like they're a group of people who feel responsible for that particular outcome.

Reflection questions

1. What ideas resonate with you from this chapter? What sticks out most in your mind?

2. If someone said to you, "I think the effort it takes to get Christians to work together in church teams is not worth the pain—rosters work just as well", how would you respond?

3. If you've served in a team at your church before, what have you found good about it, and what have you found hard about it?

3

A FRUITFUL TEAM LEADER

If you've made it to this point, I'm assuming you're still up for the challenge of growing as a team leader. Awesome. The next step is to think about your fruitfulness as a team leader.

By fruitfulness, I'm not referring to your 'success' or to 'ministry growth charts' (we'll get to those later). I'm referring to the core qualities of a Christian leader: the *character* of a Christian leader.

> But the fruit of the Spirit is love, joy, peace, patience, kindness, goodness, faithfulness, gentleness, self-control. There is no law against such things! ... If we live in the Spirit, we should walk in the Spirit. We should not become self-absorbed, irritating or envying each other. (Gal 5:22–23, 25–26)

This fruit is a wonderful description of Christian character traits. A fruitful Christian is someone who has given themselves over to Jesus to cultivate these traits in his or her life. These traits are not limited to *some* Christians; they are for *all* Christians—and that means they're for all Christian team leaders.

It seems unfortunately common for Christian team leaders to forget to express this fruit of the Spirit while leading. I'm unsure of why, but when some Christians get invited into leadership they start to act as though they've graduated from these spiritual baselines. It's almost as if they can't imagine being a leader *and* being gentle at the same time. They can't seem to grasp the idea that they can lead *and* be patient. Yet of all Christians, leaders especially need to be models of

Spirit-led people who exhibit this fruit. Indeed, the type of leaders Paul tells Timothy and Titus to look for are similar: they must be known to have basic Christian convictions and character (see 1 Tim 3:1–13; Titus 1:5–9). In other words, Christian leaders are qualified to lead if they exemplify godliness above all else. Our churches need team leaders who are not self-absorbed, not seeking their own glory, and not fearful of others' success. Rather, we need leaders who display the fruit of the Spirit *in the way they lead their teams*.

The seriousness of being fruitful

This is not a point to skip over lightly. If all you did as a team leader was try to express the fruit of the Spirit towards your team members—to do good for them as they serve, to love them as they strive, and to be peaceable as they fail—I'd be happy for you to put the book down now. You'd be an awesome team leader, because you'd be seeking to put your team members before yourself.

But before you jump straight in, it's important that we heed the multiple warnings given to Christian leaders if they don't exhibit this fruit. Church leaders at all levels are called to be "above reproach" (1 Tim 3:2; Titus 1:6–7), and to live lives that other Christians would do well to imitate. Unlike the secular workplace, the required baseline for Christian team leaders is to be examples of Christian character. This is why these words from 1 Timothy 5 apply to team leaders in some sense:

> If an accusation is made against an elder, don't accept it unless there are two or three witnesses. If, however, they are sinning, expose it in front of everyone so that the rest of them will fear the same. (1 Tim 5:19–20)

While team leaders don't carry the same level of responsibility as church over-seers (ministers/pastors), they do bear some responsibility within the church. As such, they also need to heed this warning.

Thus, team leaders should only be appointed to lead team members on the basis of their existing character traits; they should be people who are *already* humbly entrusting every area of their life to Jesus. Then, once appointed, if a team leader refuses to repent of sin, or sins in such a gross way that they should not be upheld as a trustworthy example to others, they should be removed, and we should explain to their team members why they were removed.

If you're going to be a team leader—great. But remember that your first and most important job as a Christian team leader is to *be a fruitful Christian*. Trust Jesus, be quick to repent, and seek to become more like him. Displaying the fruit of the Spirit is the essential job criteria for all team leaders.

Servant-hearted leaders

However, when it comes to living out this fruit of the Spirit with our team members, there does seem to be one characteristic that the Scriptures emphasize: being a *servant*. Leaders are meant to be other-person centred. Here's how Jesus puts it:

> Jesus called his disciples over and said to them, "Consider how the Gentiles' apparent leaders command them and how their great men dominate them. It should not be like this among you. Rather, whoever wants to be great among you will be your servant, and whoever wants to be your leader will be everyone's slave."[10] (Mark 10:42–43)

Notice two parallel things going on here. On the one hand, Jesus is hinting at the idea that he is the true servant himself. Because when you think about it, Jesus is the one who makes himself "everyone's slave". Jesus puts the world's needs before his own and goes to the cross. Jesus lays down his life to serve everyone. On the other hand, Jesus is also the one who is "great among" all—he is their *leader* even while he says this to them. And we know the one speaking these words is the eternal Son for whom and through whom all things exist (Col 1:16). Jesus commands the wind and the waves, and he commands his disciples, and he commands us. Jesus is not just one of the "great men"; he is the greatest.

Jesus is the true servant, and yet, he is still the boss.

In true Jesus fashion, he himself is the perfect model of how we are to think about leadership. Jesus lays down his life as a servant for us, but that does not mean we are the lord of him. He is not at our beck and call; we are at his. He is still the boss. He calls the shots. And yet he calls the shots that are best for us—*even at his own expense.*

This framework for Christian leadership calls for amazing humility. If you're

---

10   When Jesus uses the word "slave", he is not endorsing slavery (see 1 Tim 1:10). Rather, he's referring to the known reality of ancient slavery at that time to make a point about how he intends to lead us.

going to be a team leader, Christ calls you to follow him and make yourself a servant of your team members. He calls you to do what is best for them—*even at your own expense*. That's what servant-hearted leadership really looks like. An other-person-centred leader is someone who sees themselves as a servant to their team, but that doesn't mean you simply do what they say. You go out of your way for them, but that doesn't mean they are your boss. That's the heart of servant leadership.

What does this look like in practice?

Let me tell you what this does not mean: being a servant of your team does not mean you jump in and do everything for them. This is a common mistake first-time team leaders make. They know they're meant to be a servant to their team members, and so the moment one of their team members seems uncertain of what to do, the leader thinks, "Oh, they must need my help—I'll do it for them!" Or when there's some job that needs to be done, and no-one's been appointed to that task yet, the team leader thinks, "I could ask one of the team to do it—but I'm meant to be their servant. So I won't put an extra burden on them; I'll just do it so my team doesn't have to."

That's not serving your team, because you're not helping them do the ministry; you're stepping in and getting between them and the ministry. And while there *might* be times for a leader to do this, it should be the exception, not the norm. What your team really needs is a leader who is great at helping the team do the ministry for themselves.

Be the leader they need

Here's the big principle behind all the ideas I'm going to present in this book: *serve your team by being the team leader they need you to be* (not necessarily the team leader they *want* you to be). In fact, let's take that principle one step further: be the team leader they need *in the moment*. Whatever the moment requires you to be for them, be that.

This means the style of leadership they need from you will change from moment to moment, from issue to issue, and from season to season. Your leadership style will need to change to suit them. Team leaders need to ask ourselves, "What does my team need from me right now?"

Asking yourself this question will impact how you relate to your team in all kinds of ways—from your tone of voice, to the things you ask them to do. It will help you work out if you need to have a long conversation or send a quick text message. It will help you push forward, or slow down, or take control, or sit back and watch. Those aspects of how you lead are all up for grabs depending on what the team needs from you. The amount of freedom you give them, or the limits you set for them, will be an expression of what is *best for them in the moment*.

Paul is a good example of this principle. In 1 Thessalonians 2, he reminds his readers how at some points he was like a mother caring for them (v 7), and at other points he was like a father exhorting them (v 11). Yet he was never pretending to be someone other than who he was (vv 5–6). He was the leader they needed him to be in the moment. He made himself their servant, to lead them as they needed to be led.

This is similar to parents adapting the way they care for their children, because children get older and change. If a parent made school lunches for their child in Year 1 and is still making their lunches in Year 9, that suggests the parent hasn't changed their style to suit the circumstances.

This idea taps into one of the pain points we discussed earlier: being a team leader brings changes to your relationships with people—but it's not just a one-time change where you flip a switch and become a team leader. How you lead, and how you relate to team members, will evolve over time. Sometimes you'll find yourself taking on a parent role, but then it will become a pastoral role, then a counselling role, then an authoritarian role, then a supportive role. Sometimes you will be a shoulder to cry on, and other times you will be a captain issuing orders. You may even find that each team member needs you to be a different style of leader at the same time—perhaps one person needs encouragement, while another needs correction. There is an ideal leadership approach to every situation.

But what type of leader does your team need you to be? What types of leadership styles are there to choose from? And how do I know which one to use at any given moment? These are great questions—and, if we're honest, they might also feel like overwhelming questions! How can one leader be all these things for their team? That's exactly what we're going to consider in the rest of the book. We'll get a lot more practical, but we'll also keep things simple. There are lots of techniques and ideas we can employ to lead and serve people well. And in the end, you have God's Spirit in you; he'll help you love people like he does.

But before we get to the practical stuff, let's pray about it. Read over this prayer, and if it expresses something you want to say to God, pray it right now.

> Dear Father,
> I want to be a good team leader for the sake of my team, my ministry area and your kingdom. So please help me do two things. First, please help me to always display the fruit of the Spirit as I support my team to serve others. And second, please help me be the type of leader they need me to be in any given moment. Amen.

I'm praying this for you too.

Reflection questions

1. Why do you think Christians often forget to live out the fruit of the Spirit when they become leaders? Why might you forget?

2. What's confronting about seeing yourself as a 'servant' to your team members? What aspects of yourself will be the hardest to give up for the sake of your team?

3. How do you feel about the idea of 'being the leader they need you to be'? You could write down the name of each member of your team and spend some time considering what type of team leader would suit their personality and their circumstances.

4
—

THE FOUR CONVERSATIONS TOOL

There are loads of tips and ideas out there about how to manage people and lead teams well. Some of them are very helpful—there's a chapter at the end with some tools that my church has used over the years. But there is one tool that we've found amazingly simple and helpful.

First, though, what do I mean by a 'tool'?

When it comes to leading a team, so much of what leaders do is *think* and *speak*. That's it. Consider the soccer coach or basketball coach on the sideline during a game—they don't touch the ball, and they don't go on the court. They watch, they see things, they make decisions and they communicate them to their players. In a similar way, ministry team leading is primarily a job that involves *consideration* and *communication*. Watch and have words. Inquire and influence.

So, when I talk about a 'tool', I'm talking about something that helps you *consider* and *communicate* well with your team. A leadership tool is a way of looking at a situation which helps you to *think* and *speak*. Other words for this would be a 'paradigm' or a 'framework'.

The one leadership tool I want to help you grasp is 'the four conversations'.

The four conversations

Every interaction you have with your team members will probably fall into one of these four conversation types:

1. Let me keep you in the loop about something I'm deciding.
2. Let's chat about something I'm deciding.
3. Let's chat about something you're deciding.
4. Keep me in the loop about something you're deciding.

That's it. Whenever you're talking to one of your team members, you're probably having one of these four conversations.[11] For example:

- You've had to change the date of the social event? That's probably going to be a type-1 conversation: you're keeping your team in the loop about something you've decided.
- You want to brainstorm some ideas for your Christmas lesson? That'll probably be a type-2 conversation: you want to chat about something you're deciding.
- You want to hear where the team's up to with their weekend-away plans and make sure they understand what's important? That's a type-3 conversation: you want to chat and share your principles about something they are deciding.
- You're just checking in on the team before the youth group starts and want to know if anyone has any issues? That's a type-4 conversation: you want them to keep you in the loop about things they have already planned or are already deciding.

Breaking down your team-leader conversations into these four broad categories is extremely helpful as you seek to be the leader your team needs in the moment. It makes it much easier to ask yourself, "Which type of conversation am I having now? Which type of conversation does this person in front of me need me to have with them? What would be the most loving and servant-hearted way to talk with them right now?"

---

11 Paul Hersey offered a management model in his 1984 book *The Situational Leader,* and I am indebted to his work in the development of my model. Hersey's model presents team members as fairly static in their 'situations', which means leaders therefore choose to behave in a certain way towards each person most of the time. The model I'm presenting is about being aware of flexible situations and the types of conversations you're having based on what is best in the moment (rather than pigeon-holing someone to only one style of leadership).

When you simplify it down to just four types of conversation, it really helps you and your team listen, understand and work better together.

⁓ ◆ ⁓

At one staff meeting, our team found itself having a very intense discussion about an aspect of church life. There was a wide spectrum of ideas, and the conversation was a bit tense at times. During a moment of awkward silence, Richard asked: "Greg, this might seem like an odd question, but what type of conversation are we having here? Is this a 'we need to take a vote' conversation, or a 'Greg needs to decide' conversation?"

It was just the right question! Greg realized the issue straight away and said, "Thank you, Richard, I should have made that clear from the start. While I'd prefer everyone to come to a consensus about this, in the end I'm going to make a call, and whatever I decide, that's what we'll all do—together."

Immediately the tension in the room dissolved because we all understood what role we were playing in the discussion. We had clarity about what was going on, and about what would happen next. It wasn't just knowing it was 'Greg's decision' that made it better. Greg could have said, "It's a group decision, and I'll go with whatever the group decides". That would also have brought the clarity we needed in that moment.

⁓ ◆ ⁓

If you're more of a visual person, we can picture these four conversations in a diagram like the one below. On the left-to-right axis, you work out who is going to be making the final decision at the end of the conversation; is it you (the leader) or them (the team/team member)? On the top-to-bottom axis, you work out the amount of conversation that's likely to be involved: is this a quick conversation where you're just sharing information and keeping one another in the loop, or is it a longer discussion where you go back and forth sharing ideas and talk about values and principles? If it's quick, you're at the bottom: one side just keeping the other in the loop. If there's lots of conversing and sharing thoughts, you're at the top of the diagram.

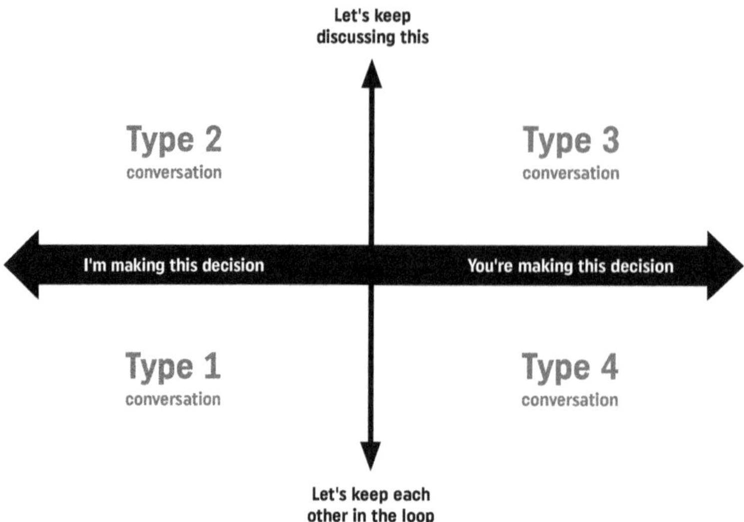

Let's look at each of the four conversation types in a little more detail (don't worry if this seems a bit quick—we'll keep coming back to these throughout the book).

Conversation type 1: "Let me keep you in the loop about something I'm deciding."

Sometimes, your team members just need you to make a decision and let them know what that means for them. That's conversation type 1. It could be telling your team the dates of the next event they're running, or telling them who's doing what jobs in kids' church next week. It might be instructing them on what things need to get set up before an event: "Gary, put out the five tables like this. Wendy, put out six chairs around each table. Frank, I want a jug of water and glasses on each table. Let's go, team!" You can also use this type of conversation to outline various team values and principles: "Hey everyone, I just want to reiterate the type of team we want to be ..."

The value of identifying this type of conversation is that it allows you to take the lead confidently and unapologetically. Many leaders shy away from using this style of communication because they feel uncomfortable simply telling their team what's going on. They pretend it's not really a direction or an instruction, or they phrase their instruction like a question ("Would it be okay if we put out five tables like this?"), as though they're asking the team to offer an opinion. But this just leads to confusion. Rather than communicating things with their team simply and directly, some leaders feel so awkward about leading that they phrase simple things in a complex way, which only leaves team members feeling confused about what is happening.

On the other hand, some leaders overuse this type of conversation. Leaders who value things being done in a specific way can end up only ever talking to their team in type 1. They find it hard to use the other three types of conversation because they just want to tell people how things should be done.

Used well, however, conversation type 1 is an excellent way to bring clarity and simplicity to some aspects of your team's work. It's all about clearly explaining to your team the simple things that have already been decided.

Conversation type 2: "Let's chat about something I'm deciding."

Sometimes, your team really needs you to be the type of leader who gets them brainstorming before you make a call on behalf of the team. That's conversation type 2. You invite your team to share their thoughts, think out loud, wonder and imagine. But an important part of this type of conversation is that you'll make the final decision. As outlined in my example above, it needs to be clear that at a certain point you'll take on board all their ideas, feedback, and comments, and *you'll* choose what *they* will do.

It's worth saying that this is a real conversation. That is, you're not pretending to listen to your team with your mind already made up. Having this type of conversation means truly opening yourself up to your team's ideas and listening to what they bring to the table. Then, and only then, you weigh up everything and make the decision for the good of the team.

Simply labelling this type of conversation enables you to discuss the values and principles you want the team to care about. We'll look at this more in a later chapter, but when your team members suggest an idea you don't like, this type of conversation is not the time to just say, "No, I don't like that". Rather, you can say, "Interesting. I'm initially hesitant to do that because one of the things that matters to me is ...", which allows you to talk about an important principle.

Like type 1, conversation type 2 is relatively simple: you invite your team members to think for themselves and you talk about their ideas, then you make the final decision.

Conversation type 3: "Let's chat about something you're deciding."

Sometimes, your team needs a leader who's going to encourage them to make their own decisions and talk through the implications of their choices. That's conversation type 3: you do lots of chatting with your team members about something they are going to decide, and you are going to follow.

Giving your team members the decision-making power does not mean dumping them in the deep end with no support or advice. What they need is help—help making their own decisions. They need support as you entrust something to them. You might say something like, "I want to chat about a decision I want you to make".

It's important that your team knows it's their decision, not yours. Let them know you will chat about it with them, and you'll share your ideas, but when it comes to the crunch you're going to trust them and let them make the call. This means you must give your authority over to them. I call this giving away your responsibility. You share the responsibility you feel for the ministry with them, and they take responsibility for some of the ministry decisions.

This type of conversation is probably the trickiest. Team members will often want to push decision-making responsibility back on to you, when what they need in that moment is a leader who helps them take that responsibility themselves. Sometimes, a team member will run ahead and make decisions when you want to have this conversation with them first. More than any other type of conversation, timing plays a big part here: choose the right time to have this type of conversation. It's too late trying to change your team's mind after the event, so you often need to plan these conversations ahead of time.

These conversations often go something like this:

> "Hey, I'd like you to oversee who's doing what in term 3, but rather than just dumping it on you, can we chat about what that means?"

> "Hey, I know you're starting to plan the end-of-year event, so can you tell me where you're up to so I could share some thoughts?"

"Hey, I know that the deadline is coming up soon, so would you like to chat through what you're thinking to help firm it up and move things forward?"

This is an important type of conversation for team leaders to learn to have: it's where you share your ideas and thoughts with some or all of your team, but the goal is that they would make the decision, not you. It's a great way to establish trust and a real sense of partnership with your team. It will also tell you a lot about how well you've trained and prepared them, and whether they're ready to take on more responsibility in the future.

Conversation type 4: "Keep me in the loop about something you're deciding."

Sometimes, your team needs a leader who lets them make decisions and just asks to be kept in the loop. This conversation type is almost always a brief chat where your team lets you know that they've made a call. Did they go with X or Y? Is everyone that we expected coming to the supper? Do I need to know about anything that's changed in the service? I don't need to chat about it, and I don't need to know why you've made the decision; I just want you to keep me in the loop about the decisions you've made.

But done well, conversation type 4 is not just checking in about *what* they've decided. It's also an opportunity to affirm your team members' decision-making authority. If you've given them the responsibility to make decisions, this is the conversation that shows them you were serious about that: it really was their decision to make. You're affirming their decision, not pulling rank and changing it (that's conversation type 1, remember?).

In other words, don't shift from this type of conversation to a conversation where you take back the decision-making authority. If they've made a call that worries you, shift into conversation type 3: "Let's chat about this decision *you're* making". That might mean saying, "Okay, that decision you made—can you tell me more about that?" Assume they have thought hard about it, and that they might have really good reasons for making that call—reasons you might not know about. Never believe you are the font of all wisdom, and always believe your team members will have things to teach you!

The conversation type they need

These four types of conversation provide an amazing clarity for both you and your team members. When you share the type of conversation you want to have, it helps them understand what you expect of them, and it keeps you from defaulting to the conversation style that you prefer.[12]

I mean it. Tell your team member what type of conversation you want to have with them. Check if that's the conversation they thought they were having. Most inter-team conflict happens because the team leader thinks they are having a type-1 conversation, while the team member thinks they're having a type-4 conversation (or vice versa).

For example, Sally is leading the Women's Bible Study team, and Tanya is responsible for providing the study materials. Sally thinks Tanya is going to bring her some options, and she (Sally) will make the final decision. But Tanya thinks she (Tanya) is making the call, because why else would Sally have asked her to spend hours preparing it? Sally thinks it's going to be a type-2 conversation, but Tanya thinks it's a type-4 conversation. Cue drama—all because they weren't clear on what type of conversation they're going to have.

I really can't overstate the importance of this. If you can agree on the *type of conversation* you're having, it will avoid a great deal of potential conflict, and pave the way to having a healthy, godly, productive conversation.

Why does this so often go wrong? One reason is because team leaders default to using just one conversation type. While it's normal to have personal preferences, remember, it's not about your preferences. You're a servant leader, right? You have to become the type of leader they need in the moment. You have to use the conversation type they need you to use, not the one you prefer.

How do you know which conversation type they need? It will usually depend on two things. *First*, do you want them to decide for themselves? *Second*, how much time do you have to talk about the issue? Look at the diagram again:

---

12   As an aside, I've also found this framework helpful as a parent of teenagers who are in a constant state of flux in working out when they should be independent and make their own decisions, and when they come under our decisions as parents. We tell them what type of conversation we want to have first, agree on that, and then have the conversation.

          THE TEAM LEADER'S HANDBOOK

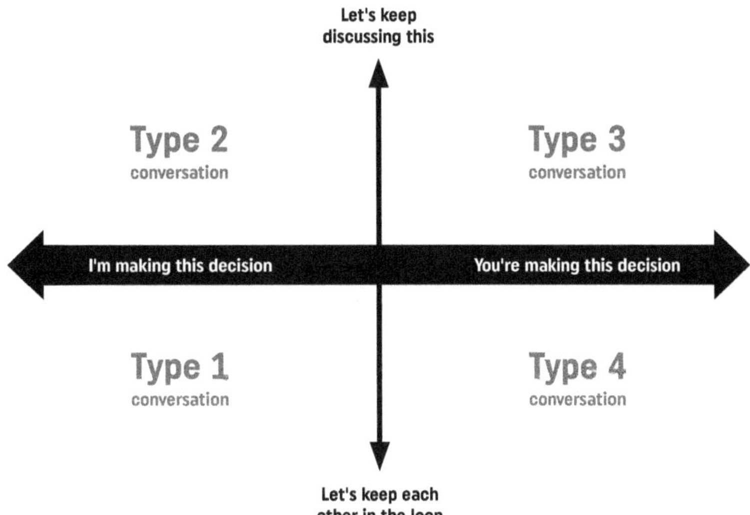

On the first point, if you are talking to a team member about something where you trust them to decide, it's best to use conversation type 3 or 4. If you don't trust them to decide, use type 1 or 2.

On the second point, if you have time for a chat where you can go back and forth and talk about the values and principles behind the decision, use type 2 or 3. If you don't have time (or you can't make time) and something is urgent, use type 1 or 4.

Let me offer one important caveat: the closer you are to the middle of the horizontal axis, the higher you need to be on the vertical axis. If the decision is sitting somewhere between you and the other person, that's a decision you need to talk about *a lot*. If you really want consensus, you need lots of time set aside to discuss the decision together. On the other hand, simply keeping each other in the loop works best when the decision is clearly yours or clearly theirs.

There will always be some topics and issues that will lend themselves to the type-1 or type-4 end of the spectrum. For example, if we're thinking about whether the Bible is the word of God and about the place it should take in influencing your team's ethics, that's not a question you want your team members to decide for themselves (even if they choose correctly). It will be a type-1 conversation.[13] In the same way, there are thousands of little decisions that your

---

13   You could certainly have a type-2 conversation about this, but there's a spectrum here, because you're not really open to being moved on some points. And that's okay.

team members will have to make—decisions that, for the most part, are not worth talking about, let alone being overly directive about. If they tell you about those little decisions, you'll probably want to keep that conversation in style 3 or 4 (even if they want the conversation to be type 1 or 2).

Talking through training

Pause for a moment and imagine how this model applies when you're trying to train someone on your team (or train your whole team) to do some *thing*. Let's say you want to train people to welcome a new family and to help get their kids into the Sunday children's program before church starts. What conversation type would you use?

First, it depends on the person you're training, right? If they already understand a lot about the systems you have in place and you just want to make sure everything is working properly, you might use conversation type 4:

> "Hey Harriet, I reckon you know most of this, but let's just go over it to make sure we're all good to go. Can you walk me through how you would welcome a new family to church? What steps would you take them through?"

This conversation is very much just getting them to give you a high-level summary of what they already think. If they say something that doesn't fit with what you want, *don't* rush to correct them (that's type 1). Instead, move the conversation from type 4 to type 3, where you invite them to talk about the principles behind their words (we'll cover this more later on):

> "You mentioned taking the kids out to the playground first. What's your thinking there? Tell me more about that."

However, if your team member is new to all this, you might start with a type-1 conversation and outline the basics:

> "Okay Adam, I'm going to walk you through the steps we want you to take when you're welcoming a new family to church. I'll run through it first, and then I'll get you to have a go, okay?"

You walk through the actions with Adam—these are all things you've already decided, and you're letting him know how he's meant to do it. You can then pause as you go and move into a type-2 conversation:

> "Okay, we've got the child to start to settle with the class. What do you reckon we might do next?"

Or perhaps:

> "So, we get the parents to fill in their contact information while their child settles in. Why do you reckon we do that? What are some of the reasons behind asking them for their details?"

Again, this allows you to have a conversation with Adam about the principles and values you want to have as a team. You can talk about the outcomes you want to work towards, and why certain things are important to the team.

All the training you'll do with your team members will basically fall into one of these four conversation types. While you might prefer to conduct training in a very type-1 way, your team might need you to train them in a more type-3 way (or vice versa). The goal is to think about your team members, consider the kind of training they might need, and work out what type of conversation is going to be best for them in that moment.

Throughout the rest of this book, I'm going to keep referring to these four conversation types. I'm going to ask you to pause and think about which type of conversation would suit various situations. Remember, team leaders are talkers. We *consider*, and we *communicate* with our team members. We get things done through our team members, and that requires talking to them—talking about what you want them to do, and discussing which things they can direct and which things you want to direct. The 'four conversations' tool is invaluable in helping you approach your team with a clearer idea of what type of talking you're going to do.

Reflection questions

1. Look at the four conversation types again. Which type of conversation comes most naturally for you as you interact with your team members?

2. If you were a team member, which type of conversation would you prefer your team leader to use with you most of the time? How would you prefer to be led?

3. Again, look at the list of people in your team. Based on what you know about them, how do you think each of them prefers to be led?

PART 2

WHAT TEAM LEADERS *ALWAYS* DO

"But what do team leaders actually do?"

Great question! The simple answer is that team leaders *consider* and *communicate*.

"Fine," you say (with a roll of the eyes), "but *what* do they consider, and *what* do they communicate?"

This answer is a bit more complicated, because it really depends on the team, the task and the team leader. There's so much that a team leader *could* consider and communicate. For example, what starts off as a seemingly small job of "lead the welcoming team on Sundays" can very quickly involve training team members, communicating with other teams in church, planning a year-long curriculum, reporting to those over you, inviting new team members to join, and removing team members who aren't faithful to their responsibilities.

So over the next three sections, I want to help you see which thinking and speaking jobs are *always* jobs, which are *sometimes* jobs, and what sits in-between. All too often, team leaders get caught up in doing things that are good but not essential. We might be caught up in helping our teams do something urgent, or we're helping solve people's problems, or we're just focused on *this week*. While there will be times when we need to attend to those kinds of issues, team leaders should always feel slightly uneasy about being 'down in the weeds', or 'out on the field' with their team.

In the next few chapters, we'll look at three things a leader should *always* be thinking and speaking about. That doesn't mean they only ever do these three things. It means, rather, that these are three responsibilities a team leader should always have in their mind, always be looking for opportunities to talk about, to discuss, to clarify. These are three things that, if you don't do them, chances are nobody else will:

1. A Christian leader always prays the big prayer.
2. A Christian leader always cultivates a gospel culture.
3. A Christian leader always focuses on principles and values.

Let's look at each of them.

5

PRAY THE BIG PRAYER

Before you start this chapter, take a minute and try to write up a 'big prayer' for your team. In one sentence, say why your team exists, but say it as a prayer.

Dear God, please help me and my ___________________ team to

____

____

____

____. Amen.

(Really. Have a go at doing this before you read on.)

You'll have a chance to revisit this at the end of the chapter, after we've thought about what goes into forming your big prayer and why this is important. But first, let's get back to our friend Steve.

Steve had resolved that he wanted to be a good team leader. He was convinced it was the best way to love the team and, in turn, to love the kids at church.

"So," Steve asked, "where do I start?"

"Well," I responded, "what type of leader do your team members need you to be? What responsibilities do they have at the moment? What do they need help with?"

Steve thought for a moment. "I don't think they really know. I think I pretty much only use conversation type 1 as a leader: I make most of the decisions and I just tell people what to do each week. They generally just do it, which is great. But they don't seem to really care about it, you know?"

I nodded, and gave Steve a moment to think. He went on: "You know, I'm not even sure my team members have a clear sense of why we're serving the kids! As I chat with them during setup and pack-up, they sometimes say some strange things."

"Like what?" I asked.

"Well, Joan's lovely, but she kept talking about how she hopes the kids get better grades at school because of the things we're doing at Kids Church. I wasn't sure what she meant, so I kind of ignored it. And then the other week, Troy said something about how it doesn't really matter what we do with the kids because we're only babysitting them so their parents can listen to the sermon. I assumed he was joking, but now that I think about it, he's always pretty reluctant to help with the class preparation."

I leaned forward on my chair and looked at him. "Steve, you know how you're having lots of type-1 conversations about *what* your team needs to do? Maybe you need to have more type-1 conversations about *why* your team exists. You know why the team exists, but maybe you need to tell them. Keep them in the loop about why they are there. Keep reminding them why you're all doing the things you're doing. At a basic level, that means getting them to pray."

"Getting them to pray?"

"Yes, your team needs to hear your prayer for Kids Church. They need to hear your prayer for the team, because that will show them what's really important about what they're doing. They need to know what you're asking God to do through them. You need to talk about your big team prayer—and then encourage them to pray those same things too."

"And that's a type-1 conversation?"

"Yes—sort of. You decide what are the key things you want your team praying for, and you keep them in the loop. Your big prayers for your team are the very reason your team exists. If your team doesn't know what you're praying for, then they won't know why they exist."

"Right", he nodded, thinking hard. There was an awkward silence. "So, what's my big prayer for Kids Church again?"

I generally dislike vision statements and mission statements. But I love prayer, and I love praying big prayers, because Scripture tells us that our God is "able to do exceedingly more than all we can ask or imagine" (Eph 3:20). Rather than focusing on vision statements and the like, I'd much rather call a team of people to pray a prayer with me, and to strive together to be part of the way God answers that prayer. This 'big prayer' doesn't need to be a formal, word-for-word prayer. It just needs to be a simple expression of what you want God to do, week in and week out, through your team.

Paul's letters in the New Testament are sprinkled with the prayers he's praying for the churches. Each prayer is a window into what he deeply values, and an invitation to pray along with his priorities. Look at one such prayer, in Philippians:

> And I pray that even now your love may grow more and more in knowledge and in all wisdom for discerning what things are excellent, in order that you may be tested and faultless on the day of the Messiah. (Phil 1:9–10)

This is Paul's vision for the people in Philippi: growing in love, growing in knowledge and wisdom—but not simply for the sake of knowing things. Paul wants them to make good decisions, to be holy, and to live lives worthy of their Lord when he comes. Paul has a vision for their lives, and so he tells them his 'big prayer'—presumably because he wants them to pray these things for themselves along with him.

A humble hope for the future

So, what should your team prayer look like? Your team prayer should present a humble and exciting vision of what you'd love God to do in your team and through your team. It's humble because it is a request, but it's exciting because you're daring to request amazing things from the king of the universe. It's what you're hoping and longing that God will make happen—either today, or this month, or next year—through your team.

As Christian team leaders, we should be asking God to work in us and through us. We should be bringing our hope for the future to God in prayer. This is the heart of our role. We are first and foremost inviting our team members to join in our prayer with us, and all their actions should flow out of that prayer. So, at its heart, your team's big prayer should paint a picture of the future you're hoping God will bring about through your labours.

A prayer with purpose

Articulating your big prayer for your team achieves several things. First, it helps renew their gospel motivation. It's normal for someone to initially say yes to serving on a church team for great gospel-hearted reasons, but after a few months when the shine has worn off the role, they can forget their initial motivation. Praying regularly, and praying big things for your team, helps reframe what they're doing as they serve.

Second, explaining your prayer for your team helps unify their overall purpose and direction. It clarifies what you are (and are not) on about. If you're not clear on the big thing you're hoping God will do through your team, that can leave your team members open to assume their own big purpose. I'm constantly surprised by the weird and wonderful 'purposes' that people assume their team is trying to achieve (e.g. they might assume serving at Kids Church is about helping the children get better grades, or just babysitting while their parents are in church).

Third, communicating your team prayer gives your team something concrete to work towards under God's grace. One of our team leaders asked his team to pray for "30 newcomers before the end of the year". As he called his team to pray for this, they started imagining what that would look like, and then started suggesting plans to make it happen. They even started to change their plans because of these 30 people they were praying for (before a single one had arrived!). There was a joyous sense of clarity brought on by asking God for a definitive outcome.[14]

Fourth, prayer lifts people's eyes from the nitty gritty of what actions they need to take, back up to the eternal effect they hope their actions will have. For example, you might want to gently shift your music team from praying about

---

14   Many Christians don't seem to like prayers that include a number, but I discuss this more in chapter 8.

how they play their instruments ("God, please help us play well") to praying about how people will engage in praise to God while they play their instruments ("God, please lift the congregation's heart and mind to Jesus as we play").

One of our apprentices excelled at this. Every week before church, he gathered the team of people who were responsible for running the meeting, and would take everyone through the same spiel every week. It went something like this:

> "Hey everyone, good to see you, let's draw it in quickly for a moment. We believe church is this hugely important event each week where God draws his people together around Jesus, and we get to serve them! Our big prayer tonight is that we'll do a great job as a team reminding people of the gospel and encouraging them to respond to God's word in heart, mind and action. Can I get someone to pray that for us now, and then we'll work through the run sheet.

Every week, the exact same thing, nearly word-for-word (I can almost still hear it). And yet it wasn't boring or rehearsed or meaningless. Every time he said it, it was obvious he deeply meant it. It took a bunch of people who'd had very different weeks filled with vastly different pressures, and called them to one single unifying thought: that what they were about to do together really mattered. And by inviting other people to pray in their own words, he was asking them to verbalize and to own those values he'd just outlined for them.

A spiritual necessity

At this point it's crucial to note that your big team prayer is not just a motivation tool, nor is it a vision statement dressed in Christian garb. It's not that you need a prayer; it's more that *you need to pray*. Praying *something* is much, much more important than 'having a team prayer'.

The whole point of having a clear prayer is first and foremost to help you and your team members to pause, quiet their hearts, come before their powerful and kind Saviour God, and ask Jesus to work through them.

In other words, please don't have a big prayer for your team simply so you can tick the box of having a big prayer. Have a big prayer *so that you pray*. And while you're praying, use the big prayer to help your team pray with you, to pray for the same things as you, and to desire the same things as each other. But even if the big prayer doesn't help your team to grasp what they're trying to do, at least you'll get them praying. And that is a more important outcome for God's children seeking to serve him together.

Which conversation type?

Let's go back for a moment and think about how we'd apply the four conversation tool here. When you talk about your big prayer with your team, which conversation type are you probably going to be using?

(Don't skip this—try to answer before you read on.)

Talking about your team prayer is almost always a conversation where you've made a decision and you're letting people know. You've decided the big prayer, and you're reminding people what it is, not asking them to weigh in on it. So that means it's almost always type 1: "I want to tell you something I've decided".

It is possible to have a longer, type-2 conversation about your big prayer. This might be something you do every year or so at an annual planning meeting. You could spend half an hour brainstorming about what they think the big prayer should be for the next 12 months, with the understanding that you will make the final decision for the team. You wouldn't want to have this conversation too regularly, because it could create a sense of instability in the team. Imagine being a team leader who asks their group every week, "Hey team, let's brainstorm together our big purpose as a team, and then I'll decide!"

Your team prayer isn't something you let your team decide for themselves. It's something you decide and remind them about. Also, it's worth mentioning that if someone's appointed you as the team leader, there's a good chance that person will want a say about your team prayer. So, make sure you check with *your leader* before you go setting a whole new direction for the ministry team you've been appointed to lead.

When Steve and I next met up, he had a notebook filled with scribbled notes and crossed out sentences. "I think I've got my team prayer!" he said, half excited and half exhausted.

"Let's hear it", I said. "In fact, why don't we pray it together?"

"Yeah", Steve replied with a smile. We bowed our heads, and he prayed, "Dear God, please use us to play a small part in the eternal life of these little brothers and sisters each week by teaching them Jesus and modelling what it means to follow him".

"Amen!" I said. "That's great! I love all the core team values you've included there. They will help your team understand a lot of the principles you care about."

"What values?"

"Well, I'm assuming when you pray for your team to 'play a small part', you're talking about how they should see themselves as partners with the parents in helping these kids grow up into Jesus. That's an important value for your team to wrap their heads around."

"Yeah, I was kinda thinking of that idea," Steve replied.

"And referring to the kids as 'little brothers and sisters' is another key idea for your team to grasp: most of these kids are part of our church family. That will shape how your team talks about them and treats them."

"I think that one just sounded right, but I do hold that value too."

"And the idea that your team should see themselves as models for these kids to follow …" I paused for Steve to finish the idea.

"Um, yeah, that's going to help my team think about how they behave at all times, even how they relate to each other."

"Yes! Part of your job as team leader is to constantly remind your team of why they exist, and of the core values and expectations that are integral to the team. You decide the prayer, the values and the expectations—and you keep explaining it to them again and again."

Writing your team's big prayer

So how do you come up with a team prayer? What should it look like?

A team prayer should be punchy, audacious and pleading. It should be punchy in that it's short, sweet and memorable—keep it to one sentence. It should be audacious in that it's a big goal—something that wouldn't happen without lots of effort and divine intervention. And it should be pleading in that it is a desperate appeal for God to work in people's lives through our efforts.[15] On top of this, your big prayer should use the words "we" and "us", not "I" and "me". This is not a prayer for you as the team leader; it's the team's prayer that *they* pray: "Father, *we* ask …", or "Father, please use *us* …", or "Father, please help *us* …"

You might not even mention your team in the prayer at all. Our church doesn't have a vision statement, but we do have a prayer: "Father, please give Jesus 30,000 people in Newy and Lake Mac—for a start".[16] This prayer doesn't even mention our own church, but it does give clarity about what we're hoping God would do—and maybe he'll even use us to make it happen.

Finally, once you've worked out your team prayer, pray it and say it. Pray it on your own. Pray it regularly, from your heart, for your team, as any Christian team leader should. But don't just pray it on your own; tell your team you're praying the prayer for them, and pray it *with* them. Ask them to start praying it together, and on their own. Cultivate a prayerfulness in your team where you all ask God to do amazing things through your efforts.

Always keep the prayer in mind

I really can't emphasize this enough. The best Christian team leaders constantly articulate what they're praying for. As they walk around their team and see people doing things, they point out how their team members' activities contribute to achieving the big prayer. They draw connections between what their team members are doing and the big prayer they've all been praying week in and week out.

In other words, when you decide the big prayer of the team, keep looking for ways to talk about it. Every time you give feedback, it's an opportunity to show how a team member's actions are connected to and support the overall team goal. And every time someone does something that you don't want them to do, you have a clear foundation upon which to talk about it. For example:

> "Hey Fred, can I chat with you about something? You know how you get the kids to play games outside? That's really helpful, because it gives them a little break to get some energy out before

---

15 One small tip is to avoid the wording "we pray …" in your big prayer. While there is nothing wrong with this wording, it can be better to use wording like "Father, please …" This can help sharpen your thinking around what you actually want God to do.

16 Newcastle ('Newy') and Lake Macquarie ('Lake Mac'), both about two hours' drive north of Sydney.

          THE TEAM LEADER'S HANDBOOK

they come in for the lesson. And remember our big prayer is that these kids would keep learning about how to love and follow Jesus. So, when the games take longer than we've planned, that means some of the kids miss out on the start of the lesson. I know they're having fun, and you look like you're enjoying it too, but remember the reason they're having a game break is to be ready and alert for the lesson. It's a key way we're trying to achieve that big prayer. Do you reckon you can help us get them all inside on time so they are ready for the lesson time?"

Again, this is an example of conversation type 1: the team leader has already written the big prayer, and she's simply reminding Fred and showing how his role contributes towards it.

The big prayer should always be on the tip of your tongue. It should be like the hum of the air conditioner—always part of the 'background noise'. Your prayer should influence everything you do as a leader, and everything your team does. A clear prayer, well articulated and regularly brought before God, may have more of an influence on your team's sense of direction and purpose than anything else. In fact, without offering a guarantee, I'd suggest that half of your team issues will probably disappear when you're all praying the same things for each other.

Your big prayer

Look back at the prayer you wrote at the start of this chapter. Is it punchy? Is it audacious? Does it plead with God to do something awesome? What changes might you want to make to it? Have another go at writing a 'big prayer' for your team.

Dear God, please help me and my _______________________ team to

____

____

____

____. Amen.

Reflection questions

1. If you asked your team what they think the big, one-sentence prayer for your team is, what do you think they'd say?

2. Share your draft big prayer with the person who oversees your leadership of your team, and ask them if it aligns with what they think your team should be praying for. What aspects do they think might be over-emphasized or under-emphasized?

3. How will you regularly pray the big prayer with your team? Where could you introduce it so they start asking God to do the same thing?

6

—

CULTIVATE A GOSPEL CULTURE

The secular approach to leading teams puts a huge emphasis on what is usually called 'team culture'. An oft-quoted phrase is "culture eats strategy for breakfast". Here, 'culture' is the unspoken habits, values and behaviours expressed by a group of people. The world around us is acutely aware of how a bad team culture can undermine the best-laid plans. And while this is observably true, the secular world doesn't have a clear idea of what really makes a 'great team culture'. Ultimately, leaders are encouraged to imagine the culture *they* want, and create the culture *in their own image*. I think the Bible might suggest there are some problems with that philosophy.

Christians have something better. We don't imagine our version of a good team culture, because ultimately it's *not our team*; it's Jesus' team. The gospel calls Christians to view themselves and each other as forgiven sinners; each of us is undeservedly declared righteous and holy by the grace of God in Christ. We serve side-by-side with those who share the same Holy Spirit, the same Saviour, the same eternal Father.

The gospel itself is our culture. The gospel of Jesus' gracious saving work and his sacrificial lordship defines the kind of culture we want in our personal lives, in our churches, in our families, and even in our ministry teams. In other words, *who* we are in Christ determines *how* we live together and serve together.

This means that a team of Christians serving together should have a culture of repentance, forgiveness and other-person-centredness, and a real sense of joy as they serve. They'll serve with gospel-shaped motivations.

We will look at these aspects of a 'gospel culture' in more detail in a moment, but first we should address the tricky question of your role as team leader when it comes to cultivating this culture.

Sharing the pastoral responsibility of team leading

One of the toughest questions of team leadership is working out how much discipleship and pastoral care you are personally expected to provide for your team members. You'll need to discuss this with your church leaders and follow their guidance.[17] But let me suggest some principles.

There are two extremes to avoid: feeling entirely spiritually responsible for your team members; or feeling zero spiritual responsibility for your team members. Let's consider these in turn.

Don't conflate 'team leader' with 'team pastor'

The first common mistake is to think that you are the team's main pastor—you have to be their sole chaplain, or their primary counsellor, or their chief Bible teacher. But this ignores the fact that you and your team members are part of a larger church community. The people in your team already have pastors who are primarily responsible for the oversight of the flock—all under Jesus, the "Chief Shepherd" of the flock (1 Pet 5:4). Look at how Paul refers to the leaders of the Ephesian church in Acts 20:

> Keep a close watch of yourselves and of the flock, among whom the
> Holy Spirit has appointed you as overseers to shepherd the church
> of God, which he purchased with his own blood. (Acts 20:28)

Notice the Holy Spirit's impact on the relationship between these church *leaders* and the church *members*: these church leaders have a responsibility to the Holy Spirit for those under their watch. The Holy Spirit knows who belongs to whom, and who is responsible for whom. This means that every member of your team already has pastors appointed by the Holy Spirit to oversee their growth. When people join your team, they do not step out from underneath

---

17   Perhaps you could even ask them which of the four conversation types they are going to use when you have this chat with them.

that oversight into your oversight. They continue as members of your church while also being in your team.

At our church, we made the decision that no-one is allowed to serve in a formal ministry team unless they are already committed to being at church regularly, and generally only if they have also committed to being a member of a small group. This ensures they have ongoing relationships with other Christians where they open the Bible and seek to grow in Christ. It also expresses one of our values: we want people to serve informally before they serve formally (i.e. love their other small-group members in many and varied ways, before loving many people in a few specific ways).[18]

Since those in your team are church members before they are team members, and since the existing church leaders are their primary shepherds (under Jesus), you do not carry the primary pastoral responsibility for them.

All Christian leadership is 'pastoral'

But at the same time, there is another extreme to avoid. This is the extreme of believing that team leaders have *zero* pastoral responsibility for their team members. After all, since your team already exists within a church community, they don't need *another* person poking around in their Christian life—right?

The problem with this view is two-fold. First, being part of a team is part of being in Christian community. All Christians have a duty to love and encourage the Christians around them. Simply by spending time with the Christians on your team, you should *want to* help them grow, mature, repent and endure. And they should want to do that for each other. That's just what Christians do to each other; you don't need to be someone's pastor to do that.

Second, any leadership within a church community carries some spiritual responsibility, because it's *leadership*. You've been appointed to *some* level of authority, and as such you share *some* level of responsibility. People are being told to follow you, your guidance, and your direction. They will inevitably look at the way you live and act and speak, and they will follow you because you're the team *leader*.

---

18 Before we instituted this (and team-based ministry along with it), we allowed anyone to volunteer their name to be on a roster. This led to some unfortunate circumstances, such as the over-zealous recruiter who invited people to be on the morning-tea roster and ended up with an unbeliever signing up to bring food and take it around after church.

What's more, you're not simply leading them to do some random action: you're leading them in service of the great and glorious Lord Jesus. Being a team leader is a way of saying, "Hey, you know how you love Jesus? Come serve him with me! I'll help you serve Jesus in a particular way, okay?" In this sense, all team leaders carry some pastoral responsibility for their team members, because they are part of Jesus' flock, and they have been entrusted to you so you can help them serve him. We can't help but care about their relationship with Jesus, and we can't help but care about their motivation to serve him faithfully and joyfully.

A shared responsibility

This means that team leaders share some pastoral responsibility for their team members, yet they do not need to feel the full weight of it all. We can thank God that our team members are already part of our church community, where the Holy Spirit has already appointed shepherds to care for them. Then, as their team leader, we get to play a small role in their Christian growth too.

One of the implications of this is that team leaders should take a real interest in their team members' participation in church. One of the best ways to help ensure the Christian growth and endurance of your team members is to piggy-back on the ways your church is already helping them. For example, how has the recent sermon series challenged your team to think about the youth ministry they're doing, or about their motivations for ministry? How has the small-group series on Ephesians made them think about what they're praying for as they serve in the kids' ministry, or how has it challenged them on their pride? What are they reading in their personal devotions, and how is it helping them approach ministry with a gospel heart?

As team leader, you don't have to start from scratch. Rather, you can come alongside the existing teaching, preaching, leadership and oversight of the church. Then, within that existing framework, express your pastoral concern for your team by helping them apply God's word to their Christian lives, especially to their service in the team.[19]

We'll talk more about what this might look like in chapter 11.

---

19   This is another reason to confirm that your team members are attending church and are committed to it before being committed to your team. This might not be such an issue in a smaller church, but as your church grows (which is what I hope you're praying for!) you can't rely on just seeing them on Sunday.

Distinctively Christian teams

It's worth mentioning another common misunderstanding when it comes to team leaders seeking to disciple their team members: it doesn't have to be you doing all the work! You can help the team to disciple the team.

That's what I mean by *cultivate a gospel culture*. Team leaders have a significant influence on the things that their teams value. If you value being on time, you won't need to say much, but everyone on the team will probably figure this out just by watching the way you operate. If you value flexibility over preparation, your team will pick up on that over time. So if you value applying the gospel to how people treat one another, your team will pick up on that. If you model being forgiving and gracious and kind and peaceable, and if you celebrate those traits in others, your team will start to value those things and celebrate them.

There's also a time and a place for being more direct—such as asking one team member to catch up with another team member. My personal goal is to lead my teams in such a way that if one of them needed encouragement or rebuke or care, the other members of the team would be the first to jump in and do that. As the team leader, I want to cultivate a culture where we all look out for each other and we all seek to care about one another's faith and growth in Christ.

This is an important element of our teams: they need to be distinctively Christian. I want my team members to see and feel a real difference between the team they are part of at work and the team they are part of at church. When they help at the local school or community centre, I want them to think, "There's something different about this team compared to my church team—the team at church is distinctively Christian. We care for each other in a special way."

There are five Christian distinctives that we should aim to cultivate in our ministry teams:

1. a culture of repentance
2. a culture of forgiveness
3. a culture of other-person-centredness
4. a culture of protecting the vulnerable
5. a culture of gospel motivation.

Let's look at each of these in some detail.

A culture of repentance

Repentance is so central to who we are as Christians that Jesus calls us to pray daily, "forgive us our sins" (Luke 11:4). This means that, unlike the world around us, Christian teams will be places of regular repentance. None of us are perfect. We have all failed in the past, and we will all fail in the future. As Christians, this is part of our identity before Jesus returns. There is no place for pride or boasting. Of all people, we should be the quickest to admit our mistakes and to take responsibility for our failures.

As leader, model this culture to your team. Be quick to repent. Be quick to admit your mistakes. You don't need to be long-winded or offer an outpouring of tears. You might say something simple like, "Hey team, I think I messed up yesterday. I can see that what I decided probably made life harder for you guys. Sorry about that." Or maybe: "I realize I didn't communicate that thing to you all before today, and I should have done that. I'll try to do better next time." Or again: "Team, I'm sorry I lost my temper and got a bit snappy in our meeting last week. I'm sorry about that—and I'll do my best to make sure it doesn't happen again."

Doing this is not only good for your own soul; it also models the type of culture you want *them* to have. When team members are quick to admit their mistakes, it helps everyone else on the team see the importance of what you're all trying to do.

A culture of forgiveness

The flip side of having a culture of repentance is encouraging your team to pray the rest of the prayer that Jesus taught: "forgive us our sins as we forgive all those who are indebted to us" (Luke 11:4). We want our teams to be places where Christians are quick to forgive one another. We don't want our teams to be places where team members hold grudges against each other—because that's not Christian.

Christians need to get better at this. All too often, I've seen or heard stories about two Christians who were volunteering on a team together, had a minor disagreement, and then ended up not speaking to each other for years. We must fight against this happening in the teams we lead. We need to prepare our teams for the reality that they *will* hurt each other, they *will* cause each other pain and frustration, and—keeping in step with the Spirit—they *will* respond with forgiveness and love.[20]

---

20 I want to strongly encourage Christians to forgive well before repentance is expressed. Jesus doesn't call us to forgive only those who have admitted their sin or asked for forgiveness. We can forgive people without raising the issue with them or requiring their admission of sin.

How do you prepare your teams for this? You talk about it up front. You have these conversations with your team *before* the issues arise. Years ago, we initiated a building committee to lead the charge in finding and developing a church property for us. We spent the first few meetings talking about how buildings and building decisions are so often the issue that tears apart churches and destroys Christian fellowship. We didn't want to be like that. Therefore, we spent a lot of time talking about the type of team we wanted to be and how we wanted to lead our church. That meant when tricky issues did come up, there was a common understanding about how Christians should deal with those issues, and we all called each other to live up to those gospel standards.

One of the key ways in which Christians should embody a culture of forgiveness is to avoid triangulating. When Ethel is frustrated with Bessie, we don't let Ethel complain about Bessie to other people. When Ethel comes to you (as the team leader) with her gripes about Bessie, don't allow her to gossip and slander. Instead, you could say something like, "Ethel, it sounds like you have some issues with Bessie that you should be raising with her before you talk to me. You don't need to 'just get it off your chest', and there's no such thing as 'godly venting'. You need to forgive her as your Christian sister, and you might need to repent of your bitterness." As Paul says in Philippians 4:

> Euodia—I exhort you! Syntyche—I exhort you! Come to an agreement. Yes, I ask you, true worker, to support these women. (Phil 4:2–3)

This is an important part of your role as a team leader. You share the responsibility (together with your church leaders) to call your team to behave Christianly towards each other, especially when they frustrate each other.

Furthermore, when they do forgive each other and express repentance to each other, that's when the team really experiences Christian fellowship. These hardships end up producing a deep sense of fellowship between your team members. Some of my closest friends are the same brothers and sisters whom I've had to forgive at great cost, and who have had to forgive me at great cost.

A culture of other-person-centredness

Christian teams will have an edge on the world around us, because we (super) naturally seek the good of others above ourselves. Remember Philippians 2:

> Do nothing according to personal ambition or self-centred pride;
> instead, value others higher than yourselves with humility. Don't
> be focused on your own interests; instead, be focused on others'
> interests. (Phil 2:3–4)

This is the attitude we want to encourage in our teams and between our team members. Even though we might assign different responsibilities to each member, we want them to care about one another's responsibilities too. We want them to care about each other. We want them to care more about the team than about themselves.

Christian teams should be places where every member is both ready to admit their own failings and to jump in and help others when they are struggling. When you see your team doing this, be quick to make a great fuss about it. Celebrate it. Make sure they know it's the type of team culture you want to cultivate.

A team of Christians serving Jesus and seeking to grow Jesus' kingdom should express gospel behaviour: quick to repent, quick to forgive each other, and less concerned about their own things than they are with the big things. That's a team with a Christian culture. That's a team that cares for each other.

A culture of protecting the vulnerable

Another thing to consider is how your team will care for the people they are serving, especially when it comes to safeguarding vulnerable people. In Isaiah, God commands: "Seek justice, stand up for the exploited, defend the orphan, and contend for the widow" (Isa 1:17). As the team leader, you have an important role to play in setting a culture where your team takes this seriously.

In most churches this will mean things like:

- Making sure your team members have completed whatever training and screening your church (and your local government) requires. It's a sad reality, but this is one of the most effective ways to help protect vulnerable people. This could mean ensuring people in your teams have answered some background questions, done a bit of training, and fulfilled any legal requirements before they begin serving. Take the time to familiarize yourself with any resources that might help with the administrative burden.[21]

---

21 For example, Safe Ministry Check (of which I am the unpaid Executive Director) is a great resource that helps Australian churches understand their legal and insurance requirements (safeministrycheck.com.au).

- Encouraging your team to avoid situations where they are alone with vulnerable people, especially children. Set a culture where the team looks out for each other. For example, if a child is sitting alone, one team member might go to check on them while another stands at the door, within eyesight, so their teammate isn't alone with the child.
- Encouraging your teams to raise concerns and showing them that you'll listen. For example, if they raise a concern about the safety of a game you're about to play at youth group, listen to them. If they have a concern that someone is being mistreated, listen to them, and if necessary help them escalate the situation to the right people in your setting.

Try to see these steps as more than just 'ticking the box' so we can get on with ministry. Viewed the right way, they are very much part of our ministry, as they help set a healthy, other-person-centred culture where we care deeply for all the people God gives us. It's also an important part of our witness to a watching world.

A culture of gospel motivation

Christians have a peculiar interest in motivations. While the world around us seems to think that motivations *can* be helpful, it doesn't really care *what* that motivation is. As long as you turn up to work and do your job well, your secular boss doesn't really care if you turn up to work motivated by a salary or a sense of duty. But Christian service is different. God cares (and therefore we care) that people are doing things for the right reasons. God does not delight in people going through the motions without their hearts being turned towards him (see Isa 1:11–17, Hos 6:6, Mic 6:6–8, Matt 6:1–18, Mark 12:29–33). God deserves not only our strength, but our hearts and minds as well.

Therefore, it's entirely possible for a Christian to serve in a team for very bad reasons. And while our motivations will never be 100 per cent pure, there are some motivations that we really must avoid.

***

Ryan was in his second year at university and had become a Christian a few months ago. He was a good guitarist, and was keen to serve in the music team. After he had joined in rehearsal for a week or two, I decided he could be in the band the following Sunday. About 30 minutes before church that week, I had a quick chat with him.

"Ryan, how are you feeling about being in the band tonight?" I asked.

Ryan seemed really excited. "I'm just happy I can finally show God how valuable I can be to him!" he said.

That wasn't what I expected to hear. My first thought was to assume he'd just chosen his words poorly, so I asked him to explain what he meant.

"Well, I was thinking, I haven't really done anything for God to love me, so if I play in the church band, that will mean I'm worth forgiving, you know? It will make me more valuable to God."

At that point, in any other organization, the team leader might think the response is a bit odd, but they wouldn't really care. Whatever motivates Ryan is fine, as long as it works. But because God cares deeply about our motivations, it would have been unloving for me to allow Ryan to go up on stage and be part of that team knowing that, in his heart, he was seeing it as a work that would make him right with God. So I told him that.

"Ryan," I said softly, "I think there are some things we need to work through before you serve in the band tonight. I don't want you to play if that's the reason you're doing it. Let's grab your gear, do church together, and we'll chat straight after. Is that okay?"

It was hard, but it was the most loving thing to do for him.

Ryan was gobsmacked. Given his motivation, he felt like I was obstructing his relationship with God. I quickly explained to the band leader what was going on, while Ryan grabbed his gear and sat up the back. I went and joined him.

When church finished, we opened the Bible and talked about God's grace. Ryan knew Jesus had cleaned the slate of his sin, but he thought he had to work up from there to be cherished and loved by God. We talked about imputed righteousness, being made holy, and being an adopted child of God who calls out "Abba, Father". We talked about how repentance and serving God are all about our response to God's grace. Being in a band is a way of saying thank you to God, not a way of earning God's favour. We talked about how the very music and songs were meant to help other people, not help us—it's an other-person-centred role.

After we'd chatted for an hour, Ryan looked at me.

"Wow, I would have been standing up there on stage for all the wrong reasons!"

"Yeah," I replied, "that's what I was afraid of. I hope you can see why I pulled you off tonight. Are you keen to give it a go next week with a new motivation?"

Ryan nodded. "Yep. Not to earn God's favour, but because of God's favour to me".

Celebrate, pray, shut down

As the team leader, you carry a shared responsibility for the motivations of your team members. You want to foster a team culture where everyone is serving Jesus, not themselves. But how exactly does a team leader foster a gospel culture? What does this look like in practice? Let me offer three practical steps: *celebrate* gospel-culture moments; *pray* for a gospel culture; and *shut down* what you don't want.

Celebrate gospel-culture moments

The first step is simply observing your team. We should always keep a tab on the team's culture, a bit like one of those computer programs that's always running in the background. During the team meetings, or during set up and pack-up, we're watching how people interact with each other. We're taking mental note of what excites the team, and what leaves the team drained. And as we do this, we're asking ourselves, "Is this how a team of people shaped by the gospel would behave?"

From there, we can ask ourselves, "How am I acting right now to help this team grasp the type of culture I think God wants us to have? How can I use this moment to communicate the type of team the gospel calls us to be?"

In other words, consider and communicate. Watch and speak. And whenever you see your team doing things that a gospel-shaped team would do, celebrate it.

When you call attention to something good, you're implicitly telling everyone to copy it. So, when you see your team accepting responsibility for mistakes, praise them publicly. When they work through a frustration together, tell them that's exactly what you hoped would happen.

I remember a staff meeting when our senior pastor held up his hand, paused the discussion, and said, "Can we just pause for a moment, because I want to point something out. There's a lot of different opinions and personal interests at stake here, and yet for the past 30 minutes as we've been thrashing this out, I can see a real desire for harmony and working hard to listen to each other. And it's beautiful. It's a testament to the Holy Spirit at work in you guys. I'm so thankful for that. Keep it up."

Not only did that help us see it in that moment; it also helped shape the way we did hard conversations for the next 12 months.

Pray for a gospel culture

Assuming that prayer is a regular part of your team's life, your team will always be extra-aware of what you pray for as their team leader. So be sure to ask God to help your team be quick to repent and forgive each other. This underlines the reality that they will need God's help by his Spirit to do it when the time comes.

When you sense your team might be coming to a moment that will test them, pause and lead them in prayer. Bring them together before God, and ask him to help you all love one another as brothers and sisters in Christ.

Shut down what you don't want

A third crucial step in establishing a gospel culture is to call out when it's gone off the rails: "Hey team, I don't think this is the way we ought to be behaving at the moment. Let's think about how God would want us to act in this situation."

When you stop a conversation, it communicates that this is the type of discussion you don't want your team to have. When someone grumbles to you about a fellow team member, asking them to stop speaking disrespectfully shows them how you think Christians should behave on your team.

Yes, this can be a hard call. It's worth using this bullet sparingly, especially with the whole team. In fact, it's almost always best to do this one-on-one. I usually start by asking the person to reflect on his or her own behaviour in the scenario. There's a good chance the Holy Spirit has already been doing his work in their heart before I get there, and they are quick to admit they should have acted differently. At that point, there's no correction or rebuke needed—just encouragement.

Love your team

Your team's gospel culture is a responsibility you share with your church or ministry organization and with your team members. As team leaders, we want to love our team members as our brothers and sisters in Christ. Firstly, this means thinking, considering and watching: is this team being Christian in their hearts and actions? Secondly, it means being the leader they need in the moment: what can I say or do right now to help cultivate and encourage this team to serve Jesus in their hearts and their actions?

In fact, let's pray for that now.

> Good Father, thanks for the godliness of the people in my team, and for the way you've already been making them more like Jesus through your Holy Spirit. Please help them to love and serve you as they serve together in this team. Help me to be a good role model in how I speak and behave. Please help me to see where they need encouragement and correction, and help me to help them, for your sake. Amen.

Reflection questions

1. When have you seen Christians own their mistakes in a ministry setting? What did they do that was helpful (or unhelpful)?

2. Are there people who you have served with on a ministry team and who have caused you pain or frustration? Are you harbouring anger or bitterness towards them, or withholding forgiveness? Or is there anyone you've wronged or hurt while serving together? What will it look like for you to repent and seek reconciliation with them?

3. Where have you already seen your team show real care for each other? How have they stepped in and shared one another's burdens on the team? How will you encourage them for this behaviour?

7
—

FOCUS ON PRINCIPLES
AND VALUES

When many people think about a team leader, the image that comes to mind is an army sergeant barking orders at his troops, or a ship's lieutenant issuing commands to the sailors on deck. The image (and often the experience) of a team leader is someone who gives instructions to their team, and watches to see that they get it done.

Using the conversation tool we looked at earlier, this is a team leader who *only* uses conversation type 1, and *only* uses their conversations to tell people what to do. This kind of team leader is solely focused on *practical* things: *where* things go, *when* things happen, *who* should do it, and *how* it should be done.

At one level, there's nothing wrong with focusing on these practical things with your team. After all, it might be what they need in the moment. There might be an emergency or a last-minute change that means the most loving thing you can do as a team leader is to use conversation type 1, be directive, and focus on the practicals.

But in most scenarios, this type of leadership has serious limitations. If you only talk about practical things, your team will only care about the practical things. They might not pause to consider why they are doing certain things. They may not understand the reasons behind the actions they're taking. Therefore, as soon as you have the chance, bring your team into these conversations. Stop focusing on the *practicals*, and start talking about the *principles*.

Focusing on principles means talking with your team about what *outcomes* you're hoping to achieve, what *values* you hold dear, and what underlying *standards* you care about. Principles focus more on *why* your team does things, while practicals focus more on *what* your team does and *how* it does things.

We see this many times in the New Testament, as the apostles move between command and motivation, from convictions to applications. For example, Paul writes to Timothy and starts with a simple directive for *what* Timothy should do: "stay in Ephesus to command certain people not to teach false doctrines ..." (1 Tim 1:3). But he quickly follows up with the motivation, the *why*, behind Timothy's action: "The purpose of this command is love, springing from a pure heart and a good conscience and sincere faith" (v 5). The result is that Timothy now has a better idea of *how* to do the former because of the latter. As he goes about the job of commanding "certain people not to teach false doctrines", he needs to do it in such a way that upholds the principle of doing it out of love and always with "a pure heart". The *why* always influences the *how*.

The why-how spectrum

You could distribute every decision and action that your team does along a spectrum where the big principles are at one end, and the small practical details are at the other end. It might look something like this:

← Principles   *Practicals →*

Team's big prayer	Team's gospel culture	Program values and standards	Desired program outcomes	Who does what	When things are due	How things are done[22]

22 It's worth pointing out that some elements of *how* we do our ministry are very much part of our big principles. For example, in 2 Corinthians 4 Paul says, "We have renounced disgraceful, underhanded ways, refusing to practice cunning or undermine God's word. Rather we commend ourselves to everyone's conscience in the sight of God by presenting the truth" (v 2). In this respect, *how* we do our ministry is deeply bound up with our "gospel culture" and our "values and standards". As a team leader, you should take a deep interest in *how* your team does its work in this sense. When I address "how we do things" in this chapter, I'm addressing the more practical and basic level of our operations—the nuts and bolts of our ministry.

From time to time, a team leader might have to dip into the right-hand end of the spectrum (practicals), and yet even then everything they say is being influenced by the things on the left-hand side of the spectrum (principles). As a team leader issues instructions to their team about how to do things, those instructions are shaped and influenced by the team leader's own principles and values. In other words, every little decision about how something should be done is an attempt to fulfil the big prayer, express the team culture, hit the desired outcomes, and uphold an array of values and standards. Every "do that" is fuelled by a truckload of "because of this".

The goal for team leaders is to spend more time on the "because of this", and let your team work out how to "do that" for themselves.

You've probably heard the old saying 'Give a man a fish and you feed him for a day; teach a man to fish and you feed him for a lifetime'. A similar thing could be said to team leaders: 'Give your team an instruction and they might do it once; teach your team what you value and they'll work it out for themselves'.

As a team leader, it's worth considering if you spend more time giving instructions *or* sharing principles. You might get things done quickly by focusing on instructions, but your team won't be able to operate well without you.

I experienced this one year we ran a holiday kids' program and Rob came along as my helper. On the first morning, I told him where the tables should go and how to set them up. After that, Rob dutifully came in every morning for the rest of the week and reset everything just as directed. Perfect.

Until it rained on the Friday.

We had to move everything inside, and that meant Rob would need to put his tables in a different location. But Rob didn't know that. By the time I arrived, he was almost finished setting them up. He was doing the job right, but he didn't know the values we had about changing things to suit the kids if needed. That was my fault, not his. If I had spent more time talking about *why* we were putting the tables there (to help the registration process run smoothly), Rob would have seen the rain and realized that things would have to change.

The point is this: take every opportunity to talk about why you want things done a certain way. If you do this, even if only briefly, you'll end up with team members who might do something differently and for the better.

Outcomes, values and standards

Every time you organize something, you unconsciously bring some desired outcomes, some underlying values, and some assumed standards. And if you've ever experienced difficulty or frustration trying to co-organize an event with someone, it's almost always because the two of you were bringing different unspoken outcomes, values and standards.

Pause for a few seconds and imagine you were asked to organize the annual dinner for your workmates or classmates. Where might outcomes, values and standards come into the picture, and how can this help us to understand the way our ministry teams function?

Assumed standards

If this is an annual event, you might have an assumed standard based on last year—a mental expectation of what the place looks like and how the evening will go. But if someone didn't come to last year's dinner, they won't share that assumed standard—in fact, they might have a very different expectation based on their previous workplace annual dinner. If they'd been asked to organize the dinner, they'd have done things quite differently based on those different standards.

When it comes to our ministry teams, if your team members come with different standards, they will end up making different decisions.

When we talk to our teams about standards, we're talking about what's appropriate or fitting. This is what Paul addresses in 2 Corinthians 4: "We have renounced shameful and deceptive ways—working without trickery and not tampering with God's message. Instead, we stand before God as the revelation of the truth to everyone's conscience" (2 Cor 4:2). In Paul's mind, there is a way to go about ministry that befits the gospel we proclaim, and there is a way that is definitely not befitting. This is what I mean by a 'standard': it is an agreed baseline of what is acceptable.

But not every standard will be as fundamental as "don't lie". Teams can have other agreed standards about how things are done. For example, if you're leading the welcoming team you might want them to uphold a standard that "new people who came to church on Sunday get contacted before Wednesday evening". If you're leading a band, you might want your team to uphold a standard that "everyone does their own practice at home for at least an hour". Standards are a shared baseline for everyone on the team about everything from what mindset we want to have (don't lie) to how we all think the ministry should happen (let's do it this way).

If you don't have shared standards, you will have mixed results and disgruntled team members. Those who don't know the standard will feel unfairly judged, and those who think there's a standard will be annoyed that others don't uphold it.

Underlying values

For this annual dinner you're planning, you're also going to have a set of underlying values that will impact things like where you hold the event and what happens at it. If your team values professionalism and dressing well in the office, you'll probably want to find a place that is a bit special and fancy. If, however, your workplace is more casual, they might value a more relaxed and fun night out. Or it might just be the other way around: a team that works in a more formal environment might appreciate letting off steam with a more relaxed dinner, while a team that operates in a casual workplace might value the chance to get dressed up for a memorable night out. You need to know your team and its culture! Similarly, if your workplace values awards and recognition, you'll want to leave time for speeches and presentations. But if they value all employees being treated like one big family, you won't have awards and speeches—you might give everyone a gift, because it highlights that everyone's equal.

These principles hold true for ministry teams. If your welcoming team are the only people greeting newcomers at church, it might be because they don't value bringing other people along with them. You might commend them for being personally committed to the task, but you'll need to persuade them of the value of a church-wide culture of welcoming. If you have a small-group leader whose studies end up being long lectures, it probably means they value things like teaching the group and being really well prepared. These are important values, but you would also want them to have higher values around things like group discussion and group fellowship. Whatever team it is, if something's not right, it's often because team members are working from different underlying values—different from each other's values, or different from yours.

If you don't talk about what you value, your team will only hear you talk about the way you want things done. Where possible, it's better to refrain from telling people what to do or how to do it. Instead, tell them what values you care about that will influence how they do things.

Desired outcomes

Similarly, your team members will all have slightly different ideas about the desired outcomes. This can very quickly breed frustration. You see this play out in weekend sporting teams, where some players assume the desired outcome is winning the championship, while other players think it's a bit of weekend fun followed by a drink after the game. These are very different goals for people on the same team. The championship hunters will always be frustrated by the drinkers, and the drinkers will always roll their eyes at the seriousness of the champions.

Your role as the team leader is to help everyone on your team share the same desired outcomes. This might already be part of your big prayer: "Lord, please allow us to welcome 30 new people into our church family this year". That's a prayer with a clear desired outcome. Everyone on the team can see and envisage what outcome they are working (and praying) towards. But there's more to it than just numbers, because what does it really mean to "welcome ... new people into our church family"? That might mean different things to different people on the team. As the team leader, you need to help your whole team be on the same page about what you think it means. You need to describe the win, paint the picture of what good looks like, so that everyone can have the same desired outcome in their minds.

Which conversation type?

Think back to our four conversation types, and which one you'd use to talk about all these principles of outcomes, values and standards. Here they are again:

1. Let me keep you in the loop about something I'm deciding.
2. Let's chat about something I'm deciding.
3. Let's chat about something you're deciding.
4. Keep me in the loop about something you're deciding.

Which type of conversation would you use to talk about team principles? (It's worth taking a second to close the book and think about it.)

The answer will depend on the people and the circumstances, but these conversations are almost always type 2 and 3. You really need to talk about principles, not just state them. And you need time. It takes more than a few seconds of conversation to make sure you and your team members are on the same page. You need a little back-and-forth, and you need to hear them state the principles in their own words to see if you've explained what you mean. You need time and relational connection to make sure they own the principles for themselves (and are not just parroting back what they think you want to hear).

That's what conversation types 2 and 3 are all about: lots more back-and-forth, sharing opinions, clarifying ideas, asking things like, "do you mean ...?" or "what about this?", or saying things like, "That's kind of what I mean, but maybe I'm not articulating it well", or "I think I get what you're saying, but could you try and say it another way to help me understand?"

Imagine this scenario: you're leading a team that's going to run a lunch after church, so you have a type-2 conversation with your team:

> You: Okay, what kind of foods could we do? Can you suggest some ideas to me?
>
> Adam: We could do a high-class, sit-down meal with three courses.
>
> You: I suppose we could. It kinda depends on the type of experience we want people to have.
>
> Bec: I was thinking we want people to focus on relationships and chatting together, and the food is incidental.
>
> You: Yeah, I think that's one of our key values for this event. Eating a meal together after church is meant to be an expression of us being a church family.
>
> Adam: Hmm, so rather than a sit-down meal, we should do something that is easy to grab and eat with other people. What about a share box with a range of items that people pick at while they talk?
>
> You: Oh, I like that type of idea! That really leans into that thing we were praying for: that people would get a chance to get to know one another a bit better.

Notice how the leader in this scenario keeps moving from the team member's *practical* idea to the *principle* behind the idea. That's the brilliance of having type-2 and type-3 conversations. You and your team members start thinking along the same lines.[23]

A common mind

The big idea here is that you're always looking for opportunities to talk principles with your team so that you all come to a common mind about those principles. Just as leaders always need to pray the big prayer and cultivate a gospel culture, they always need to think: "What principle do I want my team to uphold here?"

Imagine you're leading a team of youth leaders, and a team member comes to you and says, "Katie's brought a friend to youth group tonight but she's in a different grade than Katie. Should we put her in a group with Katie, or in a group with her own year group?" You could respond with your answer. But that doesn't help your team member next time. Instead, you could focus on the principles you want them to use and maybe encourage them to make that decision themselves.

> Right, so one of our big prayers is that more kids would come along, and that means tonight's a really significant night for Katie's friend. We really want her to come back next week, don't we? I think I'd want you to make that decision based on a few things: How different in age is she? Will she find it more awkward being with Katie's friends or being with kids she doesn't know? Ultimately, we'd want her to be in her grade group, but maybe that's something we can talk to her about over time. Are there enough kids in her grade group that would do a good job welcoming her? If you can try to hold all those questions in tension, I'm sure you'll make a great decision about where Katie's friend should go.[24]

23 There will even be times where the line between type 2 and type 3 becomes nicely blurry. Yes, someone—either the leader or the members—will always make the final call, and we should be careful not to make consensus our goal at the expense of genuine leadership or genuine delegation. And yet there are times when it's healthy to feel like you've decided something together: collaborating, sharing ideas, sharpening one another, and coming to a common mind.

24 You could opt to have this conversation afterwards, but there's something great about the pressure of needing to make a decision in the moment that seems to help team members feel like they play an important role in the team. Unless I thought it was really going to break them, I'd always encourage my team members to make decisions I think they can make.

This might seem like a waste of time when you could just make the call and get on with the night. But these are the moments you choose to be the leader they need, not necessarily the leader they want. They need a team leader who will help them work things out for themselves. And the more you talk about principles, the more your team members will come to a shared mind about the team as a whole. The more they have a shared mind about why they are doing the things they're doing, the more they will be able to work things out for themselves and be flexible as things grow and change.

Talking principles takes a lot of time

There's no getting around the fact that talking through principles and values with your team members takes a long time. I often get stuck because the team I'm leading is doing something urgent and they need concrete guidance from me. There's barely any time to say, "Let's pause for a moment and think about the values that are shaping this decision".

On top of that, these chats are rarely one-sided. Talking to your team members about values and principles often includes a lot of back-and-forth conversations. When you say, "I think one of the things that's important is that new people get spoken to after church", and someone on your team replies, "Yeah, but I wouldn't like someone coming and talking to me, so we shouldn't welcome everyone", there's a long conversation that will need to happen after that comment. You need time to understand why they think as they do, and they need time to understand why you think as you do.

Coming to a common mind takes a lot of time. In fact, it can take years. Team members who have been on the same team for a long time almost always understand the underlying values and principles better than newly-formed teams. So when you introduce a new member to the team, it's important to remember that they won't have all those same principles in place; they won't be running on all the same assumptions and understandings as everyone else. And you can't just write it down and tell them to "go away and read this" (although that might be a starting point for conversation), because these things are almost always best discussed, pulled apart and re-explained in new ways.[25]

---

25 See further thoughts on the seasons of team life in chapter 18.

This is an 'always' thing

As team leaders, focusing on big principles is one of the things we are always doing in the back of our minds. It's a little question that's constantly nagging us while we're watching our teams and thinking about how to lead them well: *What are the underlying standards, values and principles at work in the team right now?*

For example, when a team member arrives late, we might think to ourselves, "Maybe I haven't communicated some of our team values and standards about being on time for each other". When someone is wandering around during setup looking a bit lost, we think, "I wonder if they haven't really grasped the idea of being a team that helps each other whenever we can". When someone asks us a trivial question like, "Where do these outlines go?" we think, "Why doesn't he know this? Why can't he figure it out for himself? Maybe I haven't given the team enough direction, or I've given them too much direction and they're overly reliant on me".

We learn to look beyond the momentary issues and see the big picture. The underlying principles become our hobby horse.

So, when someone presents you with an idea to get your approval, don't just say 'yes' or 'no'. In our hearts, we want to respond with the values that shape your 'yes' or 'no'.

Now, for obvious reasons there will be many situations where you only have time to give the simple 'yes' or 'no' answer. But the point I'm making is that being a good team leader will mean we're *always* looking for the opportunity to talk about principles and values. We don't want people to just go through the motions because we've told them what to do; we want them to understand the *why* behind the decisions.

Reflection questions

1. Look again at the why-how spectrum. Where are you spending most of your time as the team leader (or what might your tendency be)?

← Principles   *Practicals →*

Team's big prayer	Team's gospel culture	Program values and standards	Desired program outcomes	Who does what	When things are due	How things are done

2. What things are you really confident that your team can do without you? Why is that? What common values and principles have they grasped as a team?

3. As you've read this chapter, you may have realized you hold some underlying values or standards, but without realizing it until now. If that's the case, try writing down these values and standards, and ask your team how they feel about them. You could also ask them to reflect on the values and standards they hold for the team.

PART 3

WHAT TEAM LEADERS *REGULARLY* DO

So far, I've focused on the things team leaders should *always* do and should *always* feel the weight of—things that should be constantly buzzing around in our heads: the team's big prayer, the team's gospel culture, and the principles that drive the team. We should never stop feeling the weight of those things as a team leader. They should be bubbling out of your lips all the time.

But from here on, I want to talk about things that you as a team leader will only do from time to time. You'll need to choose when to do these things, and how often to do them. Some of these things will need to be done regularly with our teams, others will happen when the opportunity arises, and still others will happen very rarely—maybe every year or so.

I'm laying it out like this because many team leaders find themselves spending lots of their time doing things that they should do less often, and they don't seem to have any time available to do the things their team members need them to do more often.

In this section we're going to look at things that you'll want to do *regularly*:

1. gather the team
2. delegate
3. give feedback
4. check in and catch up
5. have a bit of fun.

However, it's worth remembering that as we do these things, we never stop thinking about the big prayer, the team culture, and the values and principles behind everything.

8

GATHER THE TEAM

"Okay", said Steve, "I've got my team prayer, *and* I've been chatting with my team members about what I value, *and* I've been chatting with them and hearing their values and ideas. That's all been helpful, but the team still feels a bit lacklustre, like they're not really a team."

"Well," I said, "tell me what happens when you have a team meeting."

Steve looked at me with a slight cringe. "What do you mean by 'have a team meeting'?"

"I'm talking about when you get your whole team together. I was assuming you did that each week."

"Not really", he shrugged.

I realized I probably should have asked Steve this question much earlier. "Okay, walk me through what happens on Sunday from the moment you arrive on site."

Steve took a moment to picture a normal Sunday. "I get there with some of the gear and put it out in front of each classroom. Then the team members arrive in ones and twos, and I usually walk them to their class and check in on how they're going. Then I wait at the rego desk for the kids to arrive and I oversee check-in. Once the kids are in all their classes, I walk around and deal with any issues, which usually includes helping with afternoon tea and taking a crying baby back to its mum. When church is over, the kids get picked up. I walk around the classes, help with any pack-up issues, and say farewell to each of the team members."

I decided to model a type-2 conversation to him. "So", I asked, "what do you think might be the benefit of getting all your team members together at some point? What could that help achieve?"

He thought for a moment and replied: "I think I assumed all my team members have things to do when they arrive. I didn't think there was time for a big team meeting. But things are usually pretty chill as they arrive. So I think a meeting would help them see one another as a team that's working together."

"That's right." I decided Steve needed me to shift back into a type-1 conversation for a moment. "You need a team meeting. It doesn't need to go for an hour, and you don't need to preach a sermon at it. But if you never get your people together, they'll never really see themselves as a team. They'll only think of one another as associates who do similar jobs. And they'll constantly struggle to see the bigger picture."

"So, what do I do?" Steve asked.

Meetings often get a bad rap. But they can be a great time of team alignment and fellowship. It's worth it, and you should do it.

In fact, having a team meeting is one of the things *you decide* and then *tell your team about*—it's a type-1 conversation. But once you're in the meeting, you have lots of type-2 and type-3 conversations. Team meetings are where you invite your team to think and discuss things together, and most of the time those discussions will end with you (type 2) or one of them (type 3) making a decision based on your discussion.

So, what will that look like? A team meeting only needs a few elements to be great. You need to create a warm and fun environment, open the Bible briefly, re-pray the big prayer, review, plan and assign, train (if there's time), and communicate everything again. You won't necessarily do all these things at every meeting, and you don't need to do them in this particular order, but these are your basic building blocks.

Let's go through each one in turn.

1. Start relaxed, have fun and cultivate warmth

While Christian ministry is the most important work in the universe, we are still human. Your team members have likely come from work, or they're dealing with messy life issues, and it's always worth starting informally and getting a sense of how people are going.

I remember once running a meeting and beginning without a soft start—we just jumped straight into business. After 15 minutes, we reached the point when Pete was meant to give us an update on something, but he said, "I'm sorry, I haven't prepared my part. I've just come straight from the hospital where our daughter was in a critical condition last night." We all looked at him in shocked silence. He wasn't joking.

I felt terrible. I had prioritized some silly meeting agenda above just checking how my brothers and sisters in Christ were going.

On our staff team, the most important part of staff meetings isn't the Bible time, nor the announcements. It's lunch—hanging out together, being a family, reminding each other that we're real human beings with fears, loves, and lots going on.

So, start your meetings informal, and try to have some fun. Food often helps here.[26] It's also worth rethinking where you hold your meetings. The Kids Church team doesn't have to meet in the space where the children's ministry happens; the Conference Management Committee doesn't have to meet in a formal meeting room. You could invite the team to your home, or you could have lunch together and then do the meeting. Sometimes the best way to make meetings a bit more fun is to meet in a more fun location.[27]

2. Open the Bible together

Many team leaders avoid opening the Bible in their team meetings, and I can understand why. Simply opening the Bible with a group of Christians can quickly turn into a 90-minute activity. And while it's always valuable for Christians to discuss God's word (especially since we're serving him), it's doesn't have to take that long. Here are a few simple ways you could open the Bible *and* keep it short:

"Let me tell you something I read in the Bible this week ..."

---

26 Tip: Ask one of the team members to come up with a way to make sure there's some snacks at every team meeting.

27 See more thoughts on having team fun in chapter 12.

"Let's look at two or three verses for just a few minutes ..." (Read the verses aloud, then ask people to share something they find interesting.)

"Let's look at what was in the sermon last week ..."

"Let's read a psalm aloud and simply pray in response ..."

Opening the Bible and letting God speak into your ministry team helps to remind everyone that we all serve a greater master. For example, the finance team and I have been slowly working through Philippians, one or two verses at a time, for the past few years, and it's been a joy—regardless of whether the passage applies to our team or not.

3. Re-pray the big prayer

Take 60 seconds to remind the team why you're all there by re-praying the big prayer. You could take a moment to explain what the prayer means, or ask someone to pray the prayer for the team, or ask people to split into pairs and pray the prayer in their own words.

By inviting other people to pray it in their own words, you're asking them to verbalize their values and to express their sense of what's really important. Most importantly, it will ensure you're regularly calling on God to work through you to grow his kingdom, and it will keep you from drifting away from prayerful dependence on the Lord in your ministry.

Please don't have a meeting without re-praying the team's big prayer. It's the second-most important thing you want the team to gather around (after Jesus).

4. Review last time

This is one of the most-forgotten elements of team meetings. Leaders often feel awkward about asking their team to reflect on how things went 'last time'. Yet looking back is one of the best ways to get people in the right headspace for 'this time'. It opens the floor for people to brainstorm about the values that shape the team, gives the team space to own up to any issues, and maybe even receive a bit of praise from their peers.

As I write this, there's a group in the next room who just ran our Connect

Series session for newcomers. After they finished farewelling people and cleaning up, they sat down and the team leader said, "So, how did that go?" They wanted to have an immediate debrief and reflect on what went well, what needed to change, and what conversations they need to have this week before the next session.

If you never ask your team to review how things have gone, you'll never get a clear sense of what they think is good or not good. A common conversation I have with other team leaders goes like this:

Them: My team just keeps making the same mistakes week after week!

Me: Have you told them that?

Them: Well, no. But these are *obvious* things. *Simple* things. Surely they know things aren't meant to go like that.

Me: Well, maybe. Why don't you ask them how *they* think it went?

Them: But what if they think it went well?

Me: Then you can ask them why they think that, and you can tell them what you think.

This can be as simple as asking the team, "Okay, think back to last time—what do you remember?" If you want to go deeper, ask questions like:

- What's something encouraging that happened?
- What went well that we want to do again?
- What would we change or improve?
- What did you see other team members do well? What encouraged you?

If you have a record of the tasks assigned from the last meeting, you could go through them for a quick status update. Again, these are all great type-2 discussions.

If your team runs a regular ministry, there is value in doing this reflection straight after the event. But this can get a bit repetitive. So there's also value in occasionally asking your team to think back over the last few months to get a wider perspective.

If your team is meeting to plan a future event (like an an annual conference), this 'review' part of the meeting is when you ask people to share what they've done since the last meeting. It could be as simple as saying, "Let's go round the table and share the one big thing you've been working on since our last meeting". But try not to dip into the next part of the meeting as you do this. Keep it focused on the past for now.

5. Plan and assign

This is the moment you help bring clarity to what your team will be doing in the next hour, next day, next month, or next term. If possible, you (or someone in the team) should bring a draft plan to the meeting for everyone to work through together. You might make changes to that plan—or you might even throw the whole plan out the window. That's fine. But it's almost always best to start with something compared to nothing. Something—even something bad or half-baked—helps sharpen the team's focus.

How much you need to include in your plan really depends on your team and your ministry project. But I would suggest two ideas that team leaders often miss: Repetition is good; and Keep an eye on the horizon.

Repetition is good

Even if you think you've gone over the plan multiple times, that doesn't mean your team has it in their heads. If you're running Kids Church, or welcoming, or the music, or a camp, walk through the plans again. Maybe invite one team member to lead everyone else through the walk-through each time to keep it fresh. Almost every time my teams do a 'one more time' walk-through, we pick up something we'd missed.

Once you have a plan, you need to assign responsibilities to people and make sure everything is clear. This is usually the team leader's job. A type-2 conversation might look like this: "Okay, great ideas everyone. So, we've decided what we're going to do on Sunday. Jenny, can you tell Howard what we've planned? Tom, can you bring the gear? And Sue, can you prep the design elements? Great."

You could ask the team to delegate responsibilities to each other (a type-3 conversation), but generally you'll still need to ensure that everyone understands what they have been tasked to do.

Keep an eye on the horizon

It's unlikely that anyone on your team will be thinking about next month (if you're doing something weekly), or next year (if you're doing something annually). They may not even be thinking about next week! If there's something coming up in a few months, it's important to keep flagging it to your team. "Remember, we have a kids' ministry training day in May. And we need to start planning something for the weekend in June when most of us are away." If you're not keeping your eye on the horizon (or you haven't appointed someone to do that), things will spring up and surprise the team, and they'll feel like you didn't give them enough of a heads-up.

Take a moment now to think about any projects in your team's future. Do you need to put any of these projects on your team's radar? What concrete steps should you take to ensure you're prepared when the time comes?

6. Equip and train

If there's any team training and upskilling that needs to happen, this is the time to do it. You can always ask your team what training they think they might need, but in the end it's your decision (again, a type-2 conversation). Thinking about training your team is one of those things you probably can't do if you're a team member *and* a team leader at the same time. A player-coach rarely has the mental space to think about future team development. So, take this as another little push to be the type of team leader who gets off the field to be the best team leader that you can be.

It's worth pondering: If you could develop your team members in any three skills right now, what would they be? What's the next step to get one of those training sessions happening?

7. After the meeting, communicate everything again

The first thing that normally happens when a meeting ends is that everyone immediately forgets what they decided in the meeting. So, it's important to ensure someone writes it all down then shares it with the team (perhaps via email). You don't need to keep minutes or have people make formal motions. Just keep a clear record of the important things that were decided. A common way we do this is to write everything on a whiteboard as we run the meeting, then take a photo of the board and email it to everyone right then and there.

Not only does keeping a record allow your team to easily go back and remember what they said they'd do; it also communicates that the decisions you and your team made are important. If they're not important enough to write down, then the meeting doesn't sound important enough to attend.

⸻ ◆ ⸻

Team meetings can (and should) be fun experiences that help your whole team think about why they're doing what they're doing while also offering a sense of clarity about how they're all working together for Jesus.

Let's look at the six (or seven) parts again:

1. start relaxed
2. open the Bible
3. re-pray the big prayer
4. review the past
5. plan and assign
6. equip and train (if needed)
7. communicate it all again.

Remember, most of these steps are opportunities to have type-2 (or type-3) conversations. As leader, you chat with your team and genuinely listen to them and their insights, then you love them by making decisions (or you engage with them before the team makes a decision). But the whole point of the meeting is that you're inviting them into thinking for themselves, you're reminding them of the principles and values you want them to have, and you're discussing the options available. You're helping them take personal ownership of what the team does.

⸻ ◆ ⸻

I caught up with Steve after his first team meeting. "So, how'd it go on Sunday?"

"It actually went really well!" he said (sounding slightly more surprised than I'd hoped for). "I told them I wanted to have a team meeting, and this was just part of being in the team."

"Very type 1", I nodded with a smile.

"When everyone came together, we chatted for a few minutes. I even brought some special treats to make it a bit fun."

"I bet they loved that."

"Then we looked at the part of the Bible we were teaching the kids that day. I got them to chat about how it applies to us as leaders, and then I asked a few of them to pray for us. And guess what? Their prayers were really similar to the big team prayer I've been talking about over the past few weeks!"

"That means they've been taking on board some of your values."

Steve nodded enthusiastically. "Yep. We didn't really do any review of the past, because it was our first real meeting, but I told them I'd like them to watch for things to talk about next week. Then I asked each person to share what they had prepared for the day and assigned a few little things to various people. And I even remembered to tell them about the lunch we've got planned in a few weeks."

"That sounds great. Did you come up with a way to communicate it all again?"

"Yeah, I actually did—a bit different, but I'd be keen to know what you think. I sent a text to the team that night saying how much I appreciated them being on the team, and I reminded them that I'm keen to gather again next Sunday and spend some time reviewing how things have been going. I think that'll help them remember."

"Absolutely! That's a great way to show you really value their input and that you want them to take more ownership of the ministry. But you mentioned some little decisions you made during the meeting. You might want to think about how to record those too. One idea you could try is writing them up on a whiteboard as a record for the team to come back to if they forget. It's a way of showing that the decisions and assignments matter—but also that they're short-term decisions. They'll get wiped off at the end of the day. But that's up to you. I'm sure you'll think of a good idea."

Steve thought for a moment. "Yeah, that's a good idea. In fact, that will help me remember what I told people in the meeting too. I have to be honest: as soon as the meeting ended, I completely forgot who I asked to do what."

"But your team felt good having a meeting?" I checked.

"Yep", nodded Steve. "I would never have believed it!"

1. Think about the team meetings you've had with your team already. What elements covered in this chapter are you already doing?

2. What elements do you think you might want to start including? Why? How will these things help your team in its ministry?

3. What elements are you most nervous about including? For example, are you worried about a particular person taking over, or that a problem within your team might be revealed?

9

DELEGATE

If team leaders should regularly have team meetings, the next thing they should do regularly is delegate responsibilities to their team members. You'll find this is one of the most regular (and time-consuming) activities a team leader does: you look around at what needs to happen, and rather than doing it all yourself, you delegate to members of your team.

But this is more than just delegating a task. I'm talking about delegating a *responsibility*—inviting your team members (or one team member) to make some decisions for themselves.

I call this 'playing Follow the Member', because it's the reverse of 'Follow the Leader': rather than your team members following *you*, you follow *them*. You let go of a bit of control and encourage them to decide what happens next, and then you go along with it. This is the important part of having those type-3 and type-4 conversations: you make it clear that at the end of the conversation, it's their job to *choose*, and it will be your pleasure to *follow*. Don't just tell them it's their decision; tell them you'll go along with what they decide.

Team leaders often struggle here. Many begin giving tasks and small decisions to their team members, and it seems to go well—right up until one of the team members makes a decision that the team leader doesn't completely like. It's not a terrible decision, but it's not the one the leader wanted. At this point, the leader jumps in, changes the conversation back to type 1, and reverses the team member's decision.

But that's not playing Follow the Member. And it shows you never *really* delegated responsibility.

⸻ ◆ ⸻

I arrived at church a bit earlier than usual to observe as Steve led his team. They had just finished their meeting and were setting up before the children arrived. One of the team members, Dan, was responsible for the kids' check-in. I watched as Steve and Dan went to get the table and the box of gear they needed. Dan set up the table and started to unpack the gear. He spread out a tablecloth, put up a check-in sign on the wall behind him, and placed the kids' nametags in a pile on the table. Finally, he placed his chair behind the table, and sat back, waiting for the kids to arrive.

Then Steve came along and started adjusting everything Dan had done.

He flattened out the wrinkles in the tablecloth, he moved the sign slightly to the side of Dan (so parents could see it), and he neatly spread out the sheets of nametags in an orderly fashion. He even grabbed some pens for parents to use when they checked in their child. He then looked at Dan and said, "There, that looks good. Well done."

I sidled up to Steve a few minutes later and initiated a type-3 conversation.

"Steve, I noticed you felt the need to fix up a lot of what Dan had done at the rego desk. Tell me about that."

"Yeah, Dan doesn't really see all those little things, so I just do them."

"It might be that", I said. "But it could be that Dan doesn't feel responsible for them."

"What do you mean?" Steve asked.

"Well, if Dan knows that you're just going to come and fix them, then every time you do that, you're telling him that he doesn't have to care about them. Your actions are telling him that it's *not* his responsibility."

"But I want him to take responsibility for those things. He just doesn't seem to notice them."

"Steve, your role as the team leader is to help him notice those things and help him work out the best way to do it. If you don't help him understand why you value those things, then he's never going to understand why you step in and do those things."

"So, before I go to fix something, I need to stop and think why I care about it?"

"That might be a good start", I said. "And then you can talk to Dan about it. You can have a conversation with him and get him thinking about it too."

"But what if he doesn't do it the way I want it done?" Steve asked.

"Maybe you'll find that Dan comes up with an even better way. But until then, remember that it's important sometimes to step back and go along with what he thinks will work. Follow the member, and keep chatting about the decisions they're making."

⁂

'Follow the Member' means you don't take the decision away from them just because you don't like what they decided. Don't revert back to a type-1 conversation after you've had a type-4 conversation. When team leaders do that, it causes heartache for your team members. What's worse, it tells them not to trust you the next time you give them some responsibility.

I'm sure I've done this many times as a team leader, but I still remember one time I was on the receiving end. I was given the responsibility to run an evangelistic night at church. Everything apart from the date was all my decision. I gathered my team, and we planned the whole thing around some coffee cups and saucers we were going to rent for the night. The only job my leader had was to pick up the cups and saucers.

When we arrived at the venue, I found a box of mugs that were quite different from the ones we'd chosen. And there were no saucers. I asked him what happened. He replied: "Oh, I changed the order. Mugs are jazzier than cups and saucers." It was such a minor thing to him, but it was a big thing to me, because I thought it was my decision. I didn't think he should make a change without talking to me.

All too often, I've watched team leaders (including myself!) jump in and snatch a decision away from team members. Yet 99 per cent of the time, the original decision wasn't that bad, and it would have been fine to let it go; the leader simply couldn't handle watching their team do something that wasn't exactly what they wanted, so they grabbed the steering wheel while sitting in the passenger seat. Sure, the leader's preference might sometimes have been a *bit* better, but the team was far worse off, because the message delivered to the team was loud and clear: 'don't bother making decisions, because the team leader will just take over and do what they want anyway'.

So what should you do in these situations? Just go with it. Trust your team. Follow them and their decision. Choose to be the coach on the sidelines who, even though she might feel frustrated at her players, doesn't run onto the field and grab the ball herself. You can always chat about the decision later in the 'locker room', after the event, when you have a bit more perspective. In the moment, get behind them and follow their lead. Once you give them the responsibility to make the decision, follow through on your commitment to them.

And remember, there's every chance that things will go just as well—or maybe even better—than if they'd done it your way. Leading doesn't mean knowing the best way to do everything; often, it means gathering a team of people who will have gifts you don't have and will see things you don't see.

Delegate responsibilities and decisions (not just actions)

There are three levels of delegation: delegating actions, delegating decisions and delegating responsibilities.

Most leaders only *delegate actions* (or a group of actions). For example, "set up those tables", "bring a dish to share", or "prepare a study". Even though there might be some decision-making involved, the focus is completing the job. It's a little bit like how the centurion described himself in Luke 7:

> For I am also a man under authority, with soldiers appointed under
> me; I tell this one, "Go!" and he goes, and that one "Come!" and he
> comes, and my servant "Do this!" and he does it. (Luke 7:8)

It's not hard to delegate actions to your team. You just say, "Hey Jane, can you do something for me?" If Jane says yes, you tell her what you'd like her to do. If she says maybe, you tell her what you'd like her to do, and ask again, "Could you do that for me?" Delegating actions is almost always a type-1 or type-2 conversation.

The next level of delegation is to *delegate decisions*. This is where you invite someone to plan something or choose something, but they don't necessarily carry out the actions. Delegating decisions is a tricky relational dynamic, because you're giving someone authority without responsibility. Imagine a school teacher asking a parent to decide how maths should be taught in the classroom that year. It might make the parent feel involved, but who bears the weight of responsibility if it fails? The parent isn't there to see that it happens

   THE TEAM LEADER'S HANDBOOK

the way she assumed; the teacher, meanwhile, is left with a plan that might not suit her class, but she can't change it.

The unfortunate reality is that many church teams operate like this: they are invited to have *authority*, but they don't feel the *responsibility* as the ones who must carry out their own decisions. This is the problem with many elders' boards, finance committees and building teams: they have a huge control over what the church can or can't do, but they're rarely the ones who actually do the work that flows from their decisions. They're like parents who think they know better than school teachers without ever having stood in front of a class.[28]

The ideal, however, is to *delegate responsibility*. This is where we give people authority to make decisions *and* the responsibility to carry them out.

Let me offer an example. Our church recently took possession of a house we're planning to develop for ministry in a few years. That same week, a family linked to our church found themselves in a medical emergency and needed accommodation. We decided to let them stay in the house, but it was completely empty. It needed furniture. So rather than me solving that problem myself, I delegated the responsibility to someone. I chatted to Amy, a member of our church:

Me: Hey Amy, we're thinking we could let that family stay in the church house for a few months.

Amy: That's a great idea! But isn't it empty? Is there anything in there for them?

Me: No, and that's what I wanted to talk to you about. Do you reckon you could make it a home for them (and whoever uses it after them)? I can give you money to spend, and I reckon heaps of people would be keen to donate things. I can help get the word out if you want. Is that something you reckon you could take on?

Amy: (Pauses to think for a moment.) Yep, I'd love to look after that. Can I get in and have a look around to see what we need?

I wasn't giving Amy an action (get things and put them in the house), nor was I simply giving her decision-making authority (decide what goes in the house). I

28 I still believe groups like elders' boards, finance committees and building teams are important. The trick is to make sure they don't have authority over the 'practical' end of the spectrum, and instead to make them feel responsible for the 'principles' end of the spectrum (see the diagram in chapter 7).

was inviting her to take on a weight of responsibility. That means she made some decisions that I wouldn't have made, *and* she took the initiative to include some actions that I hadn't considered. For example, I assumed we'd just bring furniture in, but Amy recruited a team of people to go in and give it a good clean before the furniture arrived. Amazing!

Take a moment to ponder how your team might be different if you delegated not just actions or decisions, but *responsibility*. Imagine what they will feel like if they have the authority to make decisions *and* the responsibility to carry them out and see them through.

Delegate with the outcome in mind

So how do we delegate responsibility well? The oversimplified answer is to delegate the outcome, not the action. But what does this mean?

If you're asking a children's ministry leader to do a Bible time with the kids, don't invite them to "do the Bible time"; invite them to "help the kids understand the story". If you're asking a youth-group leader to run a game, tell them they have 15 minutes to make the kids feel semi-exhausted and yet have massive smiles on their faces. If you're asking someone to lead the church service one week, give them a picture of what they should be trying to achieve as the service leader.

In other words, when we delegate something, we should try to delegate as far to the *left* of the 'Principles' vs 'Practicals' spectrum as possible:

← *Principles*   *Practicals* →

Team's big prayer	Team's gospel culture	Program values and standards	Desired program outcomes	Who does what	When things are due	How things are done

The tricky part about delegating outcomes is getting good at describing them. There's a bit of an art to this, a certain poetry that's needed. Why? It's partly because we dance a delicate line of something called 'compatibilism', where God sovereignly uses our prayers and efforts to achieve his will. And it's partly because there are so many possible outcomes we're interested in that we don't know how to convey them simply and concisely. But as team leaders, it's important that we take the time to really think about what outcome you want to delegate to your team members and to explain it clearly to them.

One of the best examples of this is in Steven Covey's book *The 7 Habits of Highly Effective People*. Covey describes how he divided up certain household responsibilities to his children, one of whom was made responsible for the yard. Covey writes:

> I wanted him to have a clear picture in his mind of what a well cared for yard was like, so I took him next door to our neighbour's. "Look son," I said. "See how our neighbour's yard is green and clean? That's what we're after; *green and clean*."[29]

It's such a brilliant, short, punchy, memorable outcome. Since first reading Covey's example, I've tried to entrust my team members with similar pithy responsibility statements. While training up one of our pre-church setup team members, we walked around the school and I said, "Rob, we want people to *feel welcome* and *know where to go*". Everything the setup team does can be described within those two outcomes. With Amy and the relief housing, I simply asked if she could "make it a home". Another great example of this was a little plaque on the inside of the pulpit where I gave my first sermon. It read, "Sir, we would see Jesus" (taken from John 12:21). It was a wonderfully poetic reminder that the big outcome was not that I get through the sermon without throwing up, nor that people would think I was a good speaker. The outcome was that people would hear the Bible preached such that they would see and love Jesus. A little bit of poetry helps paint a thousand words.

Which conversation type?

Let's pause for a second and think about how we might use the four conversations tool as part of delegating. Look at the four conversation types again:

1. Let me keep you in the loop about something I've decided.
2. Let's chat about something I'm deciding.
3. Let's chat about something you're deciding.
4. Keep me in the loop about something you're deciding.

---

29 SR Covey, *The 7 Habits of Highly Effective People: Powerful lessons in personal change*, Free Press, 2004, p 175 (emphasis original).

Which would you use when you're delegating a responsibility to someone? (Again, take a moment to genuinely think it through.)

The answer is not straightforward. There are some elements of the conversation that seem to be type 1, such as "make it a home" or "green and clean". That is, you as the leader have already decided on the outcome you want. So does that mean it is a type-1 conversation?

To start with, yes. But then you can move it to a type-2 conversation: "What do you think I mean by 'make it a home'? What ideas spring to mind for you?" You move from type 1 to type 2 and start talking about the outcome in more detail. You talk about the values and the standards—for example: "This is how much money we have to spend ...", or "we don't want to go over the top because we're doing something different with the house in a few years", or "we don't want this to take up too much of your time or for you to feel swamped by it—I want you to give me jobs to help you".

But it doesn't stop there. At some point, you want to change the conversation to type 3, where you start talking about decisions they are going to make and enact—for example, "what do you think you'll do first?", or "when is a good time to get started?", or "what due date should you aim for?" You might even move to type-4 conversations where they are doing and deciding lots of things on their own, while just keeping you in the loop.

It's worth exploring one example in a little more detail. Picture a type-3 conversation where you ask your team (or a team member), "when do you think you can get that done by?" This is a question that invites your team, not you, to set a deadline. You invite them to look at what they've decided to do, and then to calculate how long it will take. The value of this is that it's not you imposing it on them; they are imposing a deadline on themselves. Therefore, if they don't make the deadline, they're not falling short of *your* standard; they're failing *their own* standard. It leads to a much healthier conversation: "Hey John, it seems like you thought you'd get it done by now, but you haven't been able to get to that. Tell me a bit about that. Do you think you might have set yourself too short a timeframe? Do you want to set a new deadline for yourself? Can I help you with that?"

As I mentioned at the start of the chapter, delegation takes a lot of time. It takes time to talk about the outcomes you want and the values and principles you want your team to keep in mind. In fact, you will often feel frustrated because it will take longer to communicate a delegated role than to just do it

    THE TEAM LEADER'S HANDBOOK

yourself. Because of this, team leaders often revert to delegating *actions* rather than taking the time to delegate *responsibilities*. But please recognize the importance of investing time in talking to your team members. The more you talk to them, and the more they talk to you about their responsibilities, the better team members they will be in the long run, and the healthier your whole team will be.

But what if they get it wrong?

Sometimes a team member will go a bit off the rails and make the wrong decision. How do you manage that?

Let me make this as clear as I can: *it's probably your fault.*

If a team member does something you didn't want them to do, 99 per cent of the time it's your fault. Either you've assumed they understood something when they really didn't, or you've failed to explain how important something is in your mind. So often, I've watched team members make decisions they thought were good and right, only to be met with scowls from their team leaders. But do you see the issue here? If your team members think they're making a good decision and you don't like it, you haven't helped them see the ministry through your eyes. They're team members, not mind readers.

So, how do you handle a situation where there's no time to keep discussing things, and you need to step in and save the day?

Start by saying sorry.

Apologize profusely for not explaining things more clearly, and bear responsibility for letting them make a decision you didn't want them to make. Tell them they had no way of knowing that's how you felt, and that's not their fault. You need to own it. Apologize, then gently tell them you need to make a last-minute change. If necessary because you're pressed for time, tell them you'll explain more afterwards. Then follow up as soon as possible to restore trust.

But involving yourself in this way is what we'd call the 'nuclear option'. You should only do this if the consequences of the team's decision are very serious, and there's no time to keep discussing it.

What if there is still time to have more discussion? In that case, how do you rescue the team from their own lack of judgement? I strongly recommend starting a type-3 conversation: start with positive interest, and ask them why they made their decision. Imagine being a nosy neighbour asking about what's going on in their backyard. Get the team talking. Ask them to explain how and why they arrived there. There's a good chance that they'll either have zero idea (they just plucked it out of the air), or they have grasped one key value at the expense of a few others. That is, they probably just haven't thought about it enough. So, follow up by asking how their decision reflects some of the other key values and principles you've already discussed.

At this point, your team member will probably be starting to rethink their decision. That's good, but don't undermine their confidence. Encourage them to keep talking:

> So, you've done a great job of keeping *this* principle in mind, but it's probably worth thinking more about what you want to do, especially in line with those other principles we discussed. Can you have more of a think about what *you'd like to do*. Let's keep chatting about it.

By doing this, you're keeping your team members squarely in conversation type 3, encouraging them to keep owning their decision. But you've also raised some important values and principles they have probably forgotten, but which they can now include as they rethink their idea.[30]

But in the end, the key reason why team members often make poor decisions is not because they haven't thought about it. It's because team leaders stop chatting about values and principles with them when we give them a responsibility. We move from having a type-2 conversation and skip over type-3 conversations, and instead move straight to type-4 conversations.

When you give your team members a new responsibility, don't move through the conversation types too quickly. That's not fair on them. Spend more time chatting about the big picture and your big principles, and keep talking about the decisions you want them to make.

---

30 There may be the rare time when a team member blatantly disregards your guidance and principles. That disregard of your direction is itself a failure to understand the core expectations of being
in the team, and maybe they simply haven't understood that. In this case, it might be best to have
a type-1 conversation to explain that being a team member sometimes means following directions,
and there's no way to be part of the team while ignoring the team values. Ask them if they'd like to
stay on the team and follow your lead. If not, tell them you're sorry to hear that, and if they change
their mind, they're welcome to rejoin in the future. And smile too—that often helps!

Reflection questions

1. Have you ever been told you can make a decision, only to have your leader come in and make the decision instead of you at the last minute? How did it feel?

2. What do you see as the difference between delegating an action and delegating a responsibility? What are some scenarios where this might play out in your team?

3. Which type of conversation do you normally use to delegate things to people? What would it look like for you to use another type? Have a go writing down how you might start that conversation.

4. It's easy to think delegating happens in the space of one conversation. How does this chapter challenge some of your assumptions about what it looks like to delegate something to your team?

10

GIVE POSITIVE FEEDBACK

It sounds amazingly simple and easy to do, but as I've watched loads of Christians step into team leader roles, this one habit seems to be really difficult to implement. And yet, when you start giving lots of positive feedback, it's honestly one of the most encouraging and enjoyable parts of being a team leader. So why might you find yourself watching silently when you see your team doing good things?

It could be that we don't want to annoy our team members. We see them doing something good and we don't want them to stop doing it, so we leave them to it. We assume they don't want positive feedback. But a recent survey suggested 65 per cent of employees wanted more feedback than they were getting. I think the same is true for volunteers—if not more so. Volunteers crave feedback. Your team members desperately want to know whether they're doing the things you want them to do. It's worth the odd interruption.

I think a more likely reason for our reluctance is that we assume our team members already know they're doing a good job. I see Tom go and welcome that new person—just like he's meant to do. He's obviously done that because he thinks that's a good thing to do, right? So it would just be weird for me to tell him it's good, right? In other words, we assume our team knows *that* they are doing a good job, and therefore we assume they understand *why* they're doing a good job. We think they don't need to hear it.

The problem with both of these assumptions is what happens next.

If you never give positive feedback to your team members, then you'll only ever give negative feedback to your team members. That means your team members will start to see you as the person who stands over them and shakes your head when they do something wrong.

So here's the challenge: try to give one piece of positive feedback to each of your team members this week. That's it. Just offer one piece of feedback at some point within the next seven days. Unless your team is very small, I suspect you'll find that a hard task if you're not in the habit of regularly giving positive feedback. So how do you do it?

Catch them if you can

Leadership experts Ken Blanchard and Spencer Johnson coined this wonderful phrase: "Catch people out doing approximately the right thing".[31] As soon as one of your team members does something even close to what you want them to do, let them know!

It may be hard to believe, but so often when we see our team members doing something great, at that very moment those same team members can be thinking, "Gee, I'm probably doing this wrong. I hope Dave isn't going to be disappointed." I'm constantly surprised at the number of times I've given someone feedback about something that's obviously good, only for them to respond with, "Oh, that's good! I was so unsure if I was doing the right thing or not." Sometimes, I've had to pause and take a minute just to convince them!

So if you're going to become better at giving regular feedback, don't assume your team members know when they are doing something good. How would they know if what they just did was good or not? Are they meant to read your mind? If *you* don't tell them they are doing what you want, who else will?

Here are some examples:

> Hey Hannah, can I give you some feedback? At church this morning, when you went and introduced yourself to that new family and asked them to fill in the Connect card, that was awesome. I felt so encouraged seeing that happen. And it looked like they felt really welcomed too. Great job.

> Hey Di, can I tell you something quickly? I noticed you came in early today to make sure all those flyers were printed. That was

---

31   K Blanchard & S Johnson, *The New One Minute Manager*, Thorsons, 2015, p 39.

such a thoughtful thing to do for the rest of the team, and it meant people weren't scrambling around as we started. It brought a real calmness to the morning. Great job.

Notice that these are quick conversations. It just takes a few seconds to point out how a team member has done something good. It's relatively hard to overdo this.[32] You can just sidle up to them and give them a moment that reinforces the good things you've seen them do. You don't need to wait for a prearranged meeting to discuss it.

This is one of the dangers of the 'feedback sandwich', where a leader sits down with a team member to 'sandwich' a negative comment between two positive comments they've been saving up. Why would you 'save up' giving positive feedback until you also want to give negative feedback? Just give positive feedback whenever you can.

Does this mean we never give negative feedback? What about when our team is doing the wrong thing?

It's worth shifting our perspective slightly. As discussed in the last chapter, our teams will very rarely (if ever) do 100 per cent the wrong thing. I can't think of a single example when I've seen a team member go so completely off the rails such that every aspect of what they're doing is 'wrong'. There's always some aspect of what they're doing that is 'good', even if it's just their intention to help. And there's a Christian conviction sitting behind this: we believe our team members are filled with the Holy Spirit, so we should assume that in their hearts they want to live according to the Spirit (Rom 8:4). So they're probably not trying to rebel against your leadership; they're probably just doing a poor job of trying to do a good thing. And if things go badly wrong; it's probably at least partly the leader's responsibility. Perhaps you haven't done a great job of communicating the good thing clearly.

This means it's best to think about giving *constructive* feedback rather than *negative* feedback. The goal of constructive feedback is to guide your team to reflect on what they have been doing and how they might do it differently in the future.

---

32 As I've trained and watched team leaders over the past 20 years, I can't think of any team leader who has gone overboard with the amount of positive feedback they've given out. I've seen team leaders go overboard in exuberance—people can tell when you're hamming it up. But I think you'd have to give a *lot* of positive feedback before people get tired of hearing they've done a good job.

The key here is that all feedback, both positive and constructive, is future orientated. We're not aiming to make our team members feel bad about the past; we want them to try again—but to do it a bit differently next time.

How do you give lots of feedback (whether positive or constructive)? It's worth pointing out four important elements:

1. Ask if it's a good time to receive feedback.
2. Describe the action you observed (not the motives).
3. Describe the impact of the behaviour.
4. Ask them what they think (especially if it's constructive feedback)

Ask if it's a good time to receive feedback

Simply starting with "Hey, can I give you some feedback?" is a great way to open the conversation. This helps orient your team members for the type of conversation you're having with them and prepares them for what you're about to say. Be sure to pause for a moment and read the expression on their face. Sometimes, their body language or facial expression will tell you they aren't in the right frame of mind for the conversation—especially if you're looking to give constructive feedback.

The first time you do this, your team members may be defensive because they'll assume the feedback will be negative. So be sure to do this with positive feedback to help them understand the pattern.

Describe the action you observed, not the motives

When you give feedback, comment on your team member's actions, not their intentions. Focus on behaviour, not motives.

This is the most common mistake team leaders make when it comes to giving feedback. They'll say something like, "Pete, you really loved welcoming that new family" without knowing whether Pete loved doing it. He might have found it difficult or stressful, or he might have done it begrudgingly—you don't know! We sometimes do the same thing with constructive feedback: "Jenny, it seems like you didn't really care about getting the kids' attention, and you weren't trying to connect with them". Really? How do you know what she cared about or what she was trying to achieve? Maybe she was trying very hard and she was nervous, which affected how she came across. We're not God; we cannot judge the thoughts and intentions of the human heart.

When you give someone feedback, try to tell them something specific that you observed: "Pete, I loved how you went straight up to that family with a big smile on your face". You might imagine watching an action replay of the event in your mind, and simply point out what was done well. It's amazingly simple. The same goes for constructive feedback: "Jenny, I noticed you didn't have any notes to look at towards the end of your kids' talk. Was that intentional? Sometimes you looked unsure about what you were going to say. Is that right?" Again, you're verbalizing your memory of the observable events. Even if Jenny was completely sure what she wanted to say, to you it looked like she was uncertain and lost.

Whether it's positive or constructive feedback, focusing on the actual events (rather than the assumed motives) allows you to talk about the behaviours and actions you want (and don't want) from your team.[33]

Describe the impact of the behaviour

The next part of giving feedback is telling them *why* their actions were helpful or unhelpful. *Why* was their behaviour "good"? What was *the result* of their actions? Don't just mention one thing; mention as many outcomes as you can. Draw connections between their actions and the values, outcomes and principles you want the team to hold dear. Feedback is an important way to communicate what's important to you.

This is also where you can talk about subjective feelings and perceptions, especially your own. Too often, leaders are hesitant to express how their team members' actions made them feel. But if your team members do something that you find really encouraging, why wouldn't you tell them that?[34] Most team members would love to know that the things they did put a smile on your face.

---

33 It might be that this conversation turns into a conversation about motivations. It is okay to go there, but my recommendation is to tread carefully. When you stop yourself from assuming people's motivations, it leads you to ask genuine questions. For example: "So, tell me what you were hoping to achieve there. What were the big principles you were trying to uphold?"

34 If you're giving constructive feedback, it's worth being very careful about sharing your negative feelings. Negative feelings generally weigh on people ten times more than positive feelings. You *can* use them if you really think it's going to help, but I've almost always regretted telling my team members when they've disappointed me. It's only been helpful in a few circumstances when the person struggles to naturally empathize with others. In those circumstances, I'm only telling them so they have a more rounded understanding of how their actions have affected people.

Let's look at some examples of how these first three elements could flow together, beginning with an example of positive feedback:

> "[Ask if it's a good time to receive feedback.] Hey Stu, can I give you some feedback? [Describe the action you observed.] I noticed you grabbed a few extra chairs for people during morning tea. [Describe the impact of the behaviour.] I loved that you did that. Those people didn't seem to even notice, but I thought it was a really lovely thing to do. It expressed a real other-person-centred mindset, and it meant it was much easier for those people to engage in the talk without having to stand awkwardly."

When you describe lots of outcomes, you're shaping their view of what's valuable to you as the team leader. It's a great way to shape their mindset around what you think is important.

Of course, you don't want your praise to become their main motivation, and what you think is important is not ultimately what matters most. What matters is what *God* thinks is important. Therefore, use your feedback to point directly to the gospel values at work (such as Stu's other-person-centredness). What's more, team members should be motivated not just by what's important to you, but by what's important to *them*; give feedback in a way that encourages them to share the values that are at stake. But that doesn't mean we hide our feelings either. If you thanked God for them, then tell them that too.

We can use the same model to give constructive feedback:

> "[Ask if it's a good time to receive feedback.] Hey Mark, can I give you some feedback? [Describe the action you observed.] The other day during the team meeting, I noticed a few times you leaned over and whispered something to Frank while Jenny was speaking. [Describe the impact of the behaviour.] I think the group got a bit distracted by it, and Jenny might have lost her place, or maybe even felt a bit ignored."

Notice that there's no comment about Mark's *motive*. You can't know why he was whispering, so that isn't part of your feedback. You're only commenting on the *objective* behaviour and the *subjective* impacts: "I saw *this*, and I think it led to *that*".

Ask them what they think

The last step is to invite them to think about what will happen next time. If you're giving positive feedback, this step isn't essential. You can ask them something like, "How do you think it went?" or "Do you have any thoughts?" These can be good ways to make sure they have understood what you're talking about. But I often find it's good to end with, "Great job!" or something similar.

If, however, you're giving constructive feedback, this step is very important, because this is the moment team members can take your comments on board and think out loud about how they change things in the future. This helps them own their actions and take responsibility for what they choose to do next time. In most cases, this just means saying something like:

- "Is that something you can look out for in the future?"
- "Any ideas what you might do about that?"
- "How do you reckon you might do it differently next time?"

Again, there's meant to be a positive and optimistic outlook to this conversation: it's about the future, and about how we can improve. It's not meant to be about regret, or even about saying sorry. You don't need your team members to apologize to you—although in some situations you might suggest apologizing to someone else (in the example above, you could say to Mark, "I wouldn't make a big deal of it, but it might be worth briefly apologizing to Jenny"). But even when your team members don't need to apologize to you, it still helps them to know if you wish they'd acted differently.

Which conversation type?

What type of conversation is it when we give feedback? It starts out as a type-1 conversation, but ideally it ends as a type-4 conversation. You want your team members to either continue a positive behaviour or choose a different behaviour, but you *don't* want them to start bringing you every decision they need to make. If you give feedback *and* tell them what to do next time, you're minimizing their personal responsibility and setting yourself up to become a traffic light for every future decision they make. Ensure the conversation ends with it being very clear that it's *their* decision how *they* will take this feedback on board.

You can do this right now. Think of something one of your team members did in the last few days that was good. Now pick up your phone and send them a text message:

> "Hey ________________, just reflecting on the other day and wanted to tell you how much I loved seeing you ________________________.
> That was great. So encouraging. Cheers."

Really—try sending one of these right now.

As you walk around your ministry, keep your eyes open for great things to highlight, and use them to talk about *why* they are in line with your team values. I work in an open-plan office, which means I hear one side of many ministry phone calls. Without eavesdropping on the call, I often lean over and chat after someone's finished the call. I'll say something like: "Hey, I don't know who you were talking to, but it seemed like you were making a real effort to understand them and express empathy. I think that was really good."

When I catch up with my team members and we do a mini review of some project, I'll interrupt with little comments about the good things they did and why it's important to me. At every opportunity, I want to tell my team what I like about the things they're doing, and why those things matter. It's just another way to align our values as a team.

Reflection questions

1. How are you going to give one piece of encouraging feedback to each of your team members this week? You could write a list of your team members, together with one thing each person has done recently that you appreciated.

2. Why is it important to give feedback about people's observable actions rather than their motives? Has anyone ever made an incorrect assumption about your motives? How did that make you feel?

3. What might be getting in the way of you watching and giving feedback to your team members? Do you need to do less 'on the field' so you can do more leading 'from the sidelines'?

11

CHECK IN AND CATCH UP

Most of the activities I've described so far are focused on conversations a team leader would have with their whole team. Either you're having these conversations with everyone present (i.e. a team meeting), or you're having these conversations on the fly with one or more team members as you watch them in action. But it's also important to have one-on-one conversations with team members. Team leaders should regularly arrange to check in and/or catch up with their team members individually, if possible.

But before you jump the gun and tell me there's no way you could ever have enough time for that, let me describe what I mean: I'm talking about having *some kind of individualized contact* with each member of your team *outside the regular ministry program* you do with them. *Some kind of individualized contact* could be anything from a two-hour conversation over lunch, a 45-minute chat on the phone while you drive home from work, a two-minute voice message, or a quick text message to tell them you're praying something for them.

And this doesn't have to happen every week. While it would be awesome to give as much time as possible to leading a team for Jesus' kingdom (and I highly recommend you give heaps of time to Jesus), the reality of life and responsibilities has a major impact on us and our team members. Most volunteer team leaders can only manage between one and four of these individual chats per week, depending on their circumstances and capacity. A good goal might be to try and have one of these chats with each member of your team every two months.

An important aspect of these chats is that they happen *outside the regular ministry program*. If you lead the Friday youth team, don't have this type of conversation just before the teenagers arrive, or just after they've left; this is the conversation that happens on another day of the week. If you lead the Sunday welcoming team, this is the check-in phone call that happens on Tuesday or Wednesday, not the phone call 30 minutes before they are meant to arrive.

There's two broad ways to approach this part of your ministry: the check-in conversation, and the catch-up conversation.

The check-in conversation

This type of conversation is more task-oriented and typically focuses on a specific responsibility that a team member has taken on.

The goal of a check-in conversation is threefold. *First*, you want your team member to feel supported. Start by giving them ample opportunity to raise their concerns and questions. Open the door to show that you care about them and want to help them with whatever it is they're doing. You don't want them to feel abandoned with some responsibility they don't know how to handle. The unfortunate reality is that many team members will be reluctant to tell you when they are feeling swamped or lost. They don't know how you'll react, and they don't want to feel like a failure, so they just don't speak up when they need help. That's the first reason you have the check-in conversation: you want to give your team member a chance to talk about how they're *really* going with their responsibilities.

The *second* reason for the check-in conversation is to make sure they are on track to get things done when they said they would.[35] Yes, I know, this person is probably an adult who *should* know how to manage their own time. But we all make mistakes. We all forget things or unintentionally let things slide. This conversation is a loving way to help your team member do what they said they'd do. At the same time, it might turn out that this responsibility really is too much for them and they're struggling. Or it could be that they're just stuck and don't know what to do next.

Some time ago, I asked one of our apprentices to do a kids' talk at church on

---

35   Remember, an important part of delegation is getting your team member(s) to choose the due date.

Easter Sunday. We talked about the big purpose, who it was aimed at, and how long it should be. A few days out from Easter Sunday, I did a very quick phone-call check-in: "Hey Ben, all good for Sunday morning?" I asked. "Yep", he replied. But it turns out that when Ben said "Yep", what he meant was "I have done zero work on this. I have not started writing anything, or involving other people, or even decided what I'm talking about. But I plan to do it all on Saturday night after I come home from being out with friends."

What I should have said to Ben was, "All good for Sunday morning, right? Can you tell me a bit about what you've planned?" That would have helped Ben articulate where things really stood, which would have allowed me to help him get on track. I foolishly went into the check-in conversation with a type-4 mindset ("Keep me in the loop"), not a type-3 mindset ("Let's chat").

The third reason for the check-in conversation is to make sure they are going in the right direction—not just getting the work done, but getting the work done *in the right way*. See if the outcome you're looking for is the same outcome they're looking for. Ask them about their thought process, and about what they've found difficult as they've prepared. This is another opportunity to share your values and principles, but *not* to tell them what they should do.

A common mistake team leaders make is turning a check-in conversation into a type-2 conversation: 'do it like this'. Don't become the team leader who checks in with team members to see how things are going, only to end up telling them what decisions they should make. This doesn't give the team members enough space to make their own decisions and live with the consequences. You need to work hard at keeping the conversation in type 3, where they are making the key decisions. That might even mean you avoid saying things like, "That's a great idea!" or "Yes, do that". Often these little phrases are like dog treats to team members: they get in the habit of hearing them, and they don't feel confident going ahead with any decision until they've heard you say, "Yes!". Other things you can say instead might be:

- "It sounds like you've thought really hard about this"
- "You've got some great ideas there—I'm sure you'll work it out"
- "I can't wait to see what you land on".

No matter how you decide to conduct your check-in conversation, the motivation should be to support your team member, make sure things are on track, and chat about the principles. You might meet up one afternoon to hear their youth talk and give them feedback, or you might arrange a few 10-minute phone chats over a few weeks to hear how their preparation is going. The fundamental thing is that you're initiating a conversation with them for *their* sake, about one of *their* responsibilities.

The catch-up

The other type of conversation to have with team members (outside the usual happenings of your ministry) is the 'catch up and hang out' conversation. This is a much more general conversation—an open-ended chat about the team member, the team and life in general. This is where you ask about their family, how they're finding church and who they're evangelizing at the moment. It's where you take some time just to hang out together as Christians who are interested in each other's lives. For this reason, the 'catch-up' doesn't fit easily into any of our four conversation types. If specific ministry issues come up, you might drop into one conversation type for a time. But most of the time, you can just enjoy spending time together and sharing your lives with one another.

Again, this could just be a phone call; it doesn't need to be an intense conversation over coffee or a long-winded discussion that goes until midnight. But the goal is to talk to them as a brother or sister in Christ first, not just a member of your team. In other words, this is a conversation where you show that there is more to your relationship than just being team leader and team member.

It's also worth noting that there will be unwise ways to do this. Be careful, for example, of long conversations with members of the opposite sex. If you're married and you have team members of the opposite sex, it might be best to invite them over to dinner with your spouse and get to know them as a couple. At the very least, keep open and transparent with your spouse about your conversations with your team members. Pray for them together, and ask your spouse how they think your team member might need to grow or develop in the team. My wife Julie is amazingly insightful about the women on my teams, and she's helped me do a better job of supporting them and encouraging them than I could have ever done on my own. In the same way, if you're a female leading a team with married men, it's worth making the effort to meet their spouses and get to know them as a couple.

Email and text messages

I've already mentioned that it's possible to do a check-in with a text message, and I've used messages from time to time to get to know my team members better. The reality is that many people born after the '90s don't enjoy talking on the phone and prefer conversing via messages on their phone or online. It's their native medium for relationships. So, if that's not your native medium, *become the leader they need you to be* and learn how to relate in a way that helps them.

I probably wouldn't expect the same thing from email. Email has become its own medium of communication, and it's slightly different to text messages and the like. Since email doesn't have the same expectations around immediacy, it also doesn't have the same feeling of intimacy. That is to say that email is good for information, but not as good for relationships—good for formal chats, but not for informal chats. The types of conversations I'm suggesting here are all meant to feel very informal: two people chatting about something and sharing their values and principles together. As soon as you put those things in an email, they become very hard and fixed.

Therefore, email is a better medium for communicating decisions that *have already been made*, or for clarifying things like times, dates, programs and who's responsible for what. Email is a really good way for people to write something down, or read it once, and find it again later. It's not the type of place to say, "So, how are you *really* going?"

But how?

As a team leader, you'll need to think about when and how you're going to check in or catch up with your team members. This is something you initiate with them. You can't assume they will arrange a catch-up with you if they want one. But you also don't have to catch up with everyone on the team 'equally'. Christians sometimes seem to believe they have to treat everyone in exactly the same way, like grandparents who treat their 17-year-old grandchildren exactly the same as their three-year-old grandchildren: they both get an ugly birthday card and two dollars for their birthday, and they have to sit at the kids' table. But each person on your team is different. They have different gifts, face different life pressures, and bear different responsibilities on the team. Therefore, it may be totally appropriate to catch up with one member of your team every week and another member of your team every six months, depending on their role and circumstances.[36]

If you rely heavily on one team member, it's worth touching base with them in a more regular way to make sure they're feeling supported and to help them know you have their back. Similarly, if you have a new member on the team and you're training them (because you haven't delegated that to someone else), it's worth checking in on them regularly for the first few months because there'll be lots of principles and values to make sure they understand.

There will be other differences between your catch-ups too. For example, some team members will do better with a more formal check-in: you schedule it in advance, give them a list of things you'd like to chat about, and let them know you want them to bring any questions they might have. Other team members will prefer to go for a walk together, or to chat over a coffee. When our children were young, I had a regular catch-up with one of my team members at the local supermarket while I did our family grocery shopping. He'd tell me about how things were going with his responsibilities while we walked up and down the aisles with a shopping trolley (he also came away with a much better picture of what being a dad with young kids was like—that was good for him too!).

Here's one way to work out how to check in and catch up with your team members: list their names on a sheet of paper. Circle the two or three people you think would most benefit from a check-in or catch-up. Go ahead and text them now—either to tell them you're praying for them, or to arrange a time to chat. As you get to catch up with each one, mark them off the list, and make a start with the next person. In other words, don't feel the need to do everyone all at once. This is something you plug away at over the course of a few months. Whatever system you decide to use, don't overcomplicate it. Just develop something that works for you and helps you to keep in touch with your team.

One last question

There's one simple question I wish I had asked my team members more often—a question that would have avoided countless heartaches and frustrations: "Is there anything else? Anything at all?"

---

36   I see this as an expression of the sentiment Paul talks about in 1 Corinthians 12:23.

Ask your team if there's anything they want to raise with you. When you're chatting one-on-one, or even over the phone, don't rush the end of the conversation. Be careful not to give the impression you're trying to wrap it up quickly just because you've gone through your list. Pause and ask if there's anything else on their mind that they might want to raise. This is important because when people feel nervous about saying something, they usually don't raise the issue. If they are slightly concerned that they've done the wrong thing or that there might be a problem, most people will hesitate to say anything. So, the most loving thing you can do is help them get it out. Help them feel supported, and give them the opportunity to say what they want to say.

In fact, I now start my catch-ups with this question. Before we get to any of the things I want to discuss, I ask if there's anything they want to chat about. For example: "Hey Paul, good to catch up! How's life? Tell me how things are going? Let's start with any questions or thoughts you have. Is there anything you want to go through or talk about?"

After Paul's talked about whatever is on his mind, I'll ask him my things (if they haven't already been addressed by the issues he raised), and then I'll ask him again: "Before we finish up, is there anything else you wanted to talk about? Anything at all?"

Some of the best ministry team conversations happen at this point. This may be when you really start to talk about what values you want the team to have and the real questions your team is asking. So don't forget to ask if there's anything else they want to talk about.

Reflection questions

1. If you had one hour to spend with any member of your team right now, which person would benefit the most from that time with you? Who could you catch up with that would have the biggest impact on the overall team effectiveness and team culture?

2. Are you more of a formal catch-up person or an informal catch-up person? Again, looking at the people in your team, what type of catch up would each of them prefer? How can you change to be the leader they need you to be?

3. How are you going to work out your plans to check in and catch up with your team members? What do you think will work for you and your circumstances?

12

HAVE A BIT OF FUN

I know I've already mentioned this in the chapter on gathering the team (chapter 8), but it's worth stating more generally: as a team leader, it's important to encourage your team to have a bit of fun together.

Yes, the work we're doing is some of the most important work these people will do in their week. And yes, holding out the truth of the gospel is very serious business. And yes, it is certainly possible to go too far and make 'having a bit of fun' too much of a priority. But I just don't think these are the dangers many of our church and ministry teams are facing. I think the more common danger is that people put such pressure on themselves to do things that they struggle to stop, enjoy the fellowship of being with their brothers and sisters in Christ, and serve with thanks and joy together.

This is one of the staff-team values we have at our church. We want to keep having fun together. A few weeks before writing this, one of our staff planned a staff-meeting 'takeover' where we were split into smaller groups for a one-hour treasure hunt around the city. It was great fun (even though my team got ripped off and didn't win)! It gave us a chance just to hang out and be friends in Christ in the midst of a very stressful and hectic few weeks.

It's helpful to think about your team members as a group of people who want to max out in three areas:

1. **shared purpose** (big prayer, convictions and hopes for the team)
2. **shared relationships** (they care about each other, and they have fun together)
3. **shared plans** (they know who's doing what and when it's due).

If you only have two of these elements, your team is going to feel frustrated.

If you only have a *shared purpose* and *shared relationships* but you don't have a *shared plan*, your team will feel like they're doing things, but they will stumble over each other as they try to get it done.

If you only have *shared relationships* and a *shared plan* but you don't have a *shared purpose*, your team will work well together, but they won't really know why they're doing it, which means they probably won't stay for long.

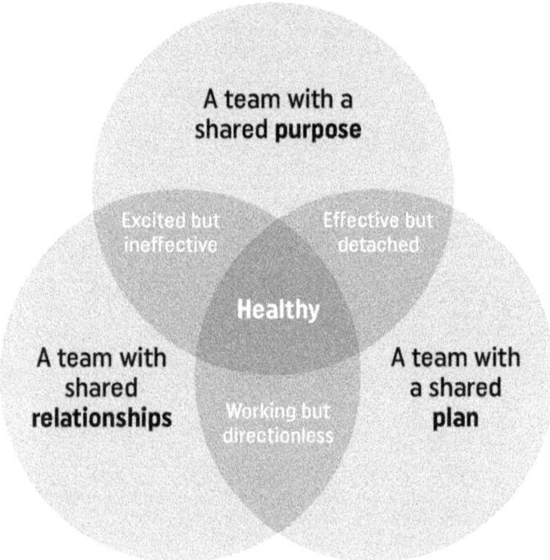

And if you only have a *shared purpose* and a *shared plan* but you don't have *shared relationships* (which I think describes most church teams), people will feel convicted and organized, but they won't enjoy serving together.

Be the champion of fun. That doesn't mean you have to lead it yourself—some of us just aren't great at that. But we can encourage certain team members to lead the way and then support them when they do it. If your team hasn't been big on fun up to this point, the first time someone leans in that direction, everyone else is probably going to glance at you to check your reaction. So, decide beforehand that you're going to get on board with the fun. Be prepared to laugh at yourself and play along. The first few times there's an opportunity to share personal things, lead the way and share something personal. Your team is going to notice if you hold back or if you lean in. The more you lean in, the more your team will be likely to follow. An important place where this can happen is in online team chat groups. Along with any ministry chat, use those spaces to share jokes or memes, or even holiday pics.

One year, our church finance team skipped the monthly meeting to have dinner and play Monopoly. It was hilarious to watch how team members handled 'play money'. Another team leader arranged to travel to a church camp with her team members and invited them to add songs to a travel playlist they listened to on the way. Our tech team played video games together, the youth team did a pizza night (without the youth), and a band leader bought coffees for everyone and the band spent 10 minutes just chatting about their week before rehearsal. A group of Bible study leaders grabbed breakfast together before work one day. These are all just examples of little ways to make the team more than functional.

An important aspect of this is to try to do something outside your normal ministry space (if possible). Simply being somewhere different helps people on your team see each other in a slightly different light. Team members become real human beings. Fellow workers become friends. Peers become people.

It probably goes without saying, but the tried-and-true method to achieve this is the simple act of opening up your home and inviting people over to share a meal. If that's going to be a stretch for you, you could always ask one of your team if they can host.

Make it more than just a transactional team. Make it a family. Make it fun.

Reflection questions

1. How does your team go having fun together? Consider the three aspects of a team, and try rating how your team fares in each one:
- shared purpose
- shared relationships
- shared plans.

2. What are some fun things you've done in a team before? Are there any you could try and encourage your team to do in the future?

3. How do you feel facilitating a bit of fun as the team leader? How does this fit with the image of being the *team coach* rather than the *team captain*?

PART 4

WHAT TEAM LEADERS *OFTEN* DO

So far in this book, we've focused on the core aspects of being a team leader: the mindset of a leader, the character of a leader, and why it's worthwhile. We've then looked at the type of things that should take up most of your time and focus: conversations about the big prayer, team culture and principles. And we've thought about the various things that should be on the team leader's regular agenda: gathering the team, delegating, giving feedback and thinking about relational dynamics.

In this next section, we will fill out our picture with some activities you should be doing *often*, or maybe *sometimes*.

But how often is *often*? And when is it *sometimes*? These are important questions that will largely depend on your circumstances and your team. But the point of using these terms is comparative: do the *often* things more than the *sometimes* things, and the *regular* things more than the *often* things—and never forget the *always* things. So, here's our list of things that you as a team leader should be looking to do often, or at least sometimes:

1. recruit new team members
2. track and report trends
3. (re)assign new roles
4. play on the team.

13

RECRUIT NEW MEMBERS

Just as a coach will often try to recruit a new player for their team, a ministry team leader will often need to recruit a new member for their crew. But why should a team leader do this? What motivates us to recruit someone new to our team?

Let's consider a few possible motivations.

There's a hole in the team

The most common reason for recruiting a new team member is because there's a need that has to be met. Either the ministry has grown and you need more helpers, or someone's moved on from the team and you need to fill their spot. Or maybe you've realized you should be delegating more responsibilities and you've run out of team members to whom you can delegate. Whatever the specific reason, this is all recruiting that's motivated by *current needs*.

There will be a hole if you grow

But there are other times when a team leader recognizes that there will be a need in the future. If the ministry or program grows like you're praying it will, then you're going to need a bigger team. You recruit now for what you hope will be required later. This is recruiting that's motivated by *future needs*.

There's an opportunity to grow

Another reason to recruit new team members is because you want to grow the ministry. For example, if a youth team had three more leaders, that might free up the rest of the team to do a better job preparing Friday nights, or chasing up new kids, or doing more evangelism in schools. If your team had 20 per cent more members, would it help you love more people better? If so, it's worth recruiting 20 per cent more members, right? This is recruiting that's motivated by *ministry potential*.

There's an opportunity to grow the person you're recruiting

A final reason you might recruit someone is because it would be good *for them*. Maybe being part of a ministry team is just the thing they need to help them feel connected at church, or to help them express their love for Jesus, or to provide them with a way to use their gifts. In other words, inviting them to be part of your team is for their good. It's a way of loving them by creating a way for them to love and serve Jesus. It's an other-person-centred thing for you to do for their good and their godliness. This is recruiting that's motivated by *pastoral love*.

Why recruit?

When it comes to recruiting new team members, most team leaders wait until they're motivated by the current need. They wait until the last minute, when there's no other option than to ask someone to step into the void. But this is the least loving thing for the new team member. They end up with no time to be eased in and trained up, yet they feel all the responsibility.

It's okay to be motivated by a need, and sometimes that will be unavoidable. But wherever possible, I want to encourage you to recruit with a different mindset—a broader motivation. Think about the future and how having a new team member *now* will help *then*. Think about how it will give you more time to get the whole team on board and to understand the big prayer and team culture. Think about how it will help them feel like part of the crew and see the ministry grow while they're there.

But most of all, I really want to encourage you to be motivated by pastoral love for the team members you're recruiting.

Invite others to serve because that's what Jesus saved them to do. This is the idea behind Ephesians 2:10: "we are God's workmanship, having been created in Christ Jesus for good works, which God preordained that we should walk in" (see also Titus 2:11–14). Not only do we as Christians have the privilege of being saved by Jesus; we also get the privilege of serving Jesus. And what does it look like to serve Jesus in church? Paul says it's all about serving Jesus' people "for the common good" (1 Cor 12:7). In other words, if you meet a Christian who's not yet serving in church, they're missing out on one of the real joys and privileges of the Christian life.

I'm pressing this point because most team leaders find it very hard to recruit new members. We don't want people to feel pressured, we don't want to put people on the spot, and we don't want to feel personally rejected if they say "no". As a result, we often delay recruitment until it's an emergency call for help. But the right mindset can help us not only have these conversations earlier; we will also have them *for the right reasons*.

When you invite someone to join the team you're leading, you are:

- inviting them to join a team that does a worthwhile ministry (I assume!)
- imagining the potential impact they might have if they joined the team (whether immediate or in the future)
- offering them the chance to enjoy the blessing of serving Jesus and his church.

These are wonderful reasons to recruit someone to your team. When you keep these reasons in the forefront of your mind, they help you to have good recruiting conversations. You will be less focused on asking for help to fill an urgent need, and more focused on what's good for the gospel, what's good for the church, and what's good for your new recruit. Rather than, "Hey, I really need someone to help on this team", it becomes, "Hey, I have an idea of how you might be able to serve Jesus on this team. Can I tell you more about it?"

Which conversation type?

Whether the potential new member is someone you know well or someone you've never met, it's worth thinking about what type of conversation you need to have with them. Often, team leaders try to have a recruiting conversation in the space of a few sentences: "Wanna join this team? No? Oh well." But the goal of a good recruiting conversation is that the potential team member makes a conscious decision *for themselves* about joining your team. They have to choose the team, rather than you choosing them.

That means a good recruiting conversation uses conversation type 3: after lots of chatting, they make the decision. Of course, you only have that conversation because you've chosen to do so. But as soon as you've decided to recruit them, it's all about what they will decide.

Your job as the team leader is to help them make a *good* decision. That means you spend a good amount of time talking with them. You might talk about the big prayer and the type of gospel culture you want the team to have. And it's not like you do all the talking! It's a type-3 conversation, so get them talking as much as possible. Yes, parts of the conversation will be type 1 (such as sharing the big prayer), and other parts will be type 2 (e.g. "Why do you think we do that?"). You might also invite them to watch the team in action and ask their own questions. But in the end, it comes down to you helping them choose for themselves by saying something along the lines of: "I'd love you to decide if you'd like to join this team".

In fact, you might get to a point where you encourage someone *not* to join your team. If you find out someone is already serving in another team, or maybe they are struggling to fulfil their existing commitments to church (not attending church or Bible study regularly), it might be best that they don't join your team. In that situation, being other-person centred means encouraging them to make other decisions, or be a better team member for someone else. Help them choose *that* for themselves.[37]

Keep recruiting your own team

This might sound odd, but you need to keep recruiting the people who are already members of your team. As the team leader, it's important that you keep inviting them to be part of the team. That might involve a formal conversation at the end of the ministry year to confirm they are going to stay on the team next year. For example:

---

37 It's worth noting you can always revoke the invitation if you decide this person shouldn't be on the team. As you talk, you might discover something which means you don't think they should be on the team. For example, you find out this person isn't coming to church regularly, or they are persisting in unrepentance, or some other character issue that is not fitting for the role. In such situations you change the conversation style to type 1 or 2. You say, "I've decided ...", and you let them know that you need to rethink the role, or that you want them to grow in character first. If you do this, it's probably worth looping in one of the pastoral staff so they are aware and can help to address the situation.

"Hey Craig, I've loved serving together with you again this year. I'd love to talk about what next year might look like for you. Can we chat about that so you can make an informed decision?"

This will usually be a type-3 conversation: you want your team members to keep choosing to be on the team. And remember, a key reason for having this conversation is because you care about them and want what's good for them. There might come a time when Craig needs to move out from being a team member to becoming a team leader himself. And he might just need that openness and support from you, his current team leader, to make that decision for himself.

On the other hand, re-recruiting your team members happens informally week by week, month by month, and throughout the whole year. Every time you talk about the team's big prayer, you are having a re-recruiting conversation with your team members. Every time you paint a picture of the future you're praying for, you're implicitly inviting your team members to be part of that future. Every time you ask them to pray for the day ahead, or for the ministry you're all doing together, you're asking them to be 'in'. It's an opportunity for them to choose again to be part of the team.

I raise this because it's not uncommon for team members to lose motivation and slowly step out of the team. People who might be feeling this way very rarely call you to say, "I'm just not feeling the team is right for me at the moment, so I'm going to pull out after this week". Instead, they just start to arrive late, or they don't arrive at all. They skip meetings and don't confirm things. And only when you happen to catch them after church one Sunday do they say, "Oh yeah, I'm probably not going to be part of that team any more" (as though they had been part of it for the past few months).

One way to protect against that type of team-member drift is to have the perspective that you're always recruiting your team, every week, into the jobs they are already doing.

Raise the next generation

Finally, it's worth pointing out that recruiting new team members isn't just about your team's needs, and it isn't just about the new recruit's opportunity to serve; it's also about the good of the church (local and global). Jesus' church needs team leaders to raise up the next generation of team leaders.

In Matthew 9, when Jesus looks out at the crowd of lost souls and feels compassion for them, he tells the disciples to "plead with the owner of the harvest so that he would send workers into his harvest" (Matt 9:38). The irony is that the disciples who heard Jesus say this probably thought *they* were the ones already being sent into the harvest. But Jesus says they should long for more workers, fellow workers, to help them. Christians who are already serving Jesus should have a righteous longing to see ever more Christians serving Jesus. We want to see all Christians serving and playing their part in the body of Christ.

One of the ways some people will express being part of the body will be through serving in your ministry team. In fact, it might be the first formal ministry they've ever done in their Christian life. Wouldn't that be awesome? When you think about it, every person who has ever served *you* as part of a formal team was once invited into service by someone else. Someone invited that person who taught you in Sunday school to serve Jesus in that ministry. The evangelist who explained the gospel to you was once asked if they'd try giving a talk for the first time. Every pastor, elder, minister and chaplain was at one point a Christian who had never been asked to serve—until someone asked them.

A hundred years from now (unless Jesus returns), there will be Christians serving the kingdom because you invited someone to serve the kingdom. The next generation of Jesus' harvest workers are called and raised up by the current generation: you.

How to recruit

Let's focus on the most common conversation: inviting someone to join your team. Here's a simple example of what you might say to begin the conversation:

> "Hey, I lead the _______________ team, and I was hoping to chat with you about possibly being part of it. Can we chat for a few minutes so I can tell you a bit about it?"

The first step is to invite them to have a conversation about it. If you jump straight into the conversation, before asking permission to have the conversation, you might find out later that they really didn't want to have the conversation right then (or at all).

From there, rather than jumping straight into a sales pitch, pause and find out a little about them first: "Before I tell you about the team, tell me a little bit about how you're going at the moment: is there anything big happening in your life right now?" Because you're motivated by pastoral love for them, take a moment to be relational and ask about them. This is often when you find out they are already serving in another ministry team, or they have just made the decision to move interstate in a few weeks. I'm constantly surprised by the number of people who don't even think to mention these things when they are asked to serve. So, take the time to ask.

Once you establish that there's some interest in joining the team, start sharing your vision for the ministry.

> "Let me tell you about the ________________ team. Our big prayer is
> ________________. That means we do things like ________________,
> and we want to do it as a team that loves Jesus and each other. Can
> you see yourself being part of a team like that?"

Obviously this part of the conversation would be longer, and you'd give them opportunities to give their thoughts and ask their questions. But there's an important part of 'the ask' here: you invite them to *join the team*, not to *do a role* on the team. The job is being a Welcome Team member, not welcoming people at the gates. The job is being a youth team member, not leading a group of teenage boys. The team, not the role, is the job.

Why? Because if circumstances change, roles will change. If the ministry grows, the roles will need to grow and adapt. But the team prayer and the team purpose remain the same. So invite them to be part of the team. That way, you're inviting them to share the big, overarching, gospel-centred vision for the work—not just to do a specific job. They might take on a particular role (to start with), but don't recruit them to the role. *Recruit them to the team.* In fact, there's an even fuller way of saying this: *recruit them to the cause of the gospel as expressed in the work of the team.*

Once you've laid out the vision and given them a chance to ask questions and share their thoughts, give them a chance to own the decision and think it over:

> "If you don't have any other questions, is this something you want to
> decide now, or would you like to take a few days to think about it?"

Don't assume people need to go away and prayerfully meditate on a decision to serve Jesus. Some people are perfectly fine with making decisions on the spot, while others really appreciate the chance to think and reflect. If so, remember to follow up with them. Don't assume they will just call you. Pursue them.

Recruiting new team members takes a lot of time. Team leaders who are swamped with leading the team are often the very ones who most need to take time out to recruit new members—which is all the more reason to keep trying to remove yourself from the team jobs and focus on being the team leader. Your team members need you to be a team recruiter for their sake. Rather than trying to give them more of your time, recruit someone else who can give their time.

Reflection questions

1. Who first invited you into serving in a formal ministry capacity? What do you remember about it?

2. Look back at the four different motivations to recruit new team members. Which motivation are you most likely to use? Which one would you prefer to be motivated by?

3. How do you feel about the idea that you are always recruiting your own team members, even while they're on the team? Are there potential dangers to this perspective?

14

RECORD, TRACK AND REPORT

I need to confess something: this is a chapter I never thought I'd put in a book on Christian team leadership. In my mind, team leadership has always been about relationships and people. It's about the team—helping the team work together to prayerfully achieve great things. I would never have thought it included tracking and reporting numbers. But I've become convinced this is one of the important ways team leaders love their team members. Coaches record their team's progress, parents record their children's growth, and team leaders record their ministry outcomes. It's a very natural expression of love and leadership.

Recording how your team's ministry is going shows that the work they are doing is valuable, it shows that their efforts are important, and it helps reinforce the aims for everyone on the team.

You count what you love, and you love what you count

In John 21, the disciples hauled in 153 fish after Jesus told them to cast their net into the water (John 21:6, 11). Why does John tell us that number? Is there some hidden message we're meant to find? No. I think Peter and John, being fishermen their whole life, couldn't help but count the huge number of fish. They were excited by it, so they recorded it! And our God seems to be similar: the Lord numbered the children of Israel (see the book of Numbers) and God knows the number of hairs on your head (Matt 10:30). And if your ministry area cares for people, then it seems odd that you *wouldn't* record the number of people you're caring for. This isn't so that you can feel boastful or proud; it's so your team can do the best possible job of loving them.

If you don't count and track things like the number of people in your ministry program, you will inevitably get the wrong sense of how many people your team is trying to serve. Here are a few examples based on real ministries I've heard about or seen:

> John leads the welcoming team and assumes that he only needs one other team member to help him because he thinks there are never many newcomers at church. But then John starts tracking the number of newcomers every Sunday. It turns out that in his church of about 100 regular attendees, there is an average of four visitors per week—about 200 visitors per year. If he split this between himself and his one team member, they'd have to follow up 100 people each. That would mean two phone calls to new people every week, plus two phone calls to follow up the people from the previous week, plus four phone calls to the people who came last month. And that doesn't leave enough room for organizing events such as lunches and welcome dinners.

> Jenny leads her church's Friday youth group, with around 15 young people usually in attendance. She starts taking a roll every week to track which kids come regularly, and she discovers that there are about 45 kids on the roll. It turns out there are about ten kids who come every week, and about 35 kids who come irregularly. She decides she needs to rearrange her team to do a better job of contacting the 45 kids during the week (with parental permission, of course), rather than having her team spend all their time preparing for Fridays when 30 of the youth aren't there.

> Paul leads a band at church on Sundays, and he thinks they're pretty good—they rarely make any mistakes. But he starts to record the songs and give them a rough score (1–5) after each set. He also asks one or two of the other band leaders at church to do the same thing. After a few weeks of keeping score and looking at the results,

Paul realizes that his band does lots of songs really well, but that they always seems to mess up one or two songs that have a particular style. Paul takes this observation to his band and asks them to help him decide if they should drop that style of song, or if they should try to work harder and get them right.

There's no doubt that it can be very hard to work out a good measure for your team and the ministry they do. How do you know if it's having the desired effect in people's hearts? You can't! But we can measure and track some things, and this is worth doing—it shows that we value what we're doing.

Something to aim for, and something to celebrate

When you record your team's outcomes and report back to them, it helps them to visualize the shared goal they are working towards. For example, if you lead the evangelism team, you can ask them to pray that God would save ten people through your church before the end of the year. That's a really clear goal. Having a number in mind helps to get the team thinking about how they will make it happen. Are they going to run a prayer night? An evangelistic series after church? Should they run a personal evangelism training course, or host a big evangelistic event for people to invite their friends to? Maybe they just letterbox drop the neighbourhood.

But it also means there's something to celebrate as you go. When the first person turns to Christ for the year, that's something you message the group about and celebrate. Answered prayer—how wonderful! Let's keep praying for nine more—at least!

Past trends shed light on future plans

But how do you come up with a number like "ten new Christians"? Is that a big number, or a small one? Why not pray for a thousand people to be saved?

While I want to encourage Christians to pray big prayers, a better approach is to look at what God has already done through your team and ask him to multiply it. If five people became Christians last year, ten people becoming Christians the next year would be amazing! But if 50 people became Christians last year, it's verging on unfaithfulness to only ask God to save ten next year. Look at the trend, and ask God to multiply that number. You can still pray for thousands, but setting a smaller goal for your team is still a way they can be part of God saving thousands.

Tell people how it's gone

I really believe in reporting back to your team, and to your church, about how things have gone. If people have been working hard and praying for something to happen, it's good and right to let them know that their prayers have been answered—or that their prayers have yet to be answered, and to ask them to keep praying.

It's also important to let your 'boss' know how it's gone. Whoever appointed you as the team leader should be told how many people have been reached, how many events have been held, or where things are up to in whatever ways are most relevant. It might be a simple email saying, "Hey, just thought I'd keep you in the loop about the Welcoming Team. Over the past three months we've had 40 newcomers attend church, and 10 of them have decided to make our church their home. Isn't that great! Let me know if you have any questions."

This will ensure that your leader knows what's happening in the team you've been appointed to lead. You should assume they want to know how things are going—they'd probably rather you give them too much information than not enough.

A good reality check

Another reason to record, track and report how your team's ministry is going is that you may need a good reality check. So often in church life, Christians persevere in repeating the same ineffective ministry program, all the while thinking that they're doing good work and it's helping people. But what if it's not? What if the youth group hasn't seen anyone become a Christian in three years? What if the small groups are only attended by 25 per cent of your church, and those 25 per cent don't attend regularly? What if you get 200 visitors every year, but only five of them join your church?

Looking at the numbers will sometimes cause a bit of pain as we start to wonder if we've been doing something wrong for a while—not morally wrong, but maybe there's a better way, and we need to take some responsibility for how things have been going. If you don't look at the numbers, you will be able to avoid asking yourself that question. But that's not good enough, because Jesus already knows how many people have slipped through the cracks. Jesus knows how many souls he sent to your church, and he knows how many weren't welcomed well or invited to look at the Bible with someone.

Refusing to look at the numbers does not mean the people they represent aren't real. If you care about the people your ministry team is trying to love, then care about every single one of them.

But how?

How do you start tracking things as a team leader? The simple answer is a spreadsheet. The better answer is that you delegate this responsibility to a member of your team who likes spreadsheets. Generally, you have one column for dates, and one column for each thing you want to track.

What you choose to track will depend on your area of ministry. Brainstorm with your team, and ask your leader what they think. Here are a few ideas to get you started:

- A regular ministry program might track newcomers' attendance, regulars' attendance, the number of people who filled in a feedback card, and maybe something else you're interested in (e.g. what time we *actually* start and end each night).
- A welcoming team might track the number of newcomers, the total number of people in attendance, the number of newcomers currently being followed up, the number of newcomers who've formally joined the church this year, and reasons why people attended but didn't join.
- A one-off ministry event might track the number of registrations one month out (compared to last year), the number of attendees (compared to last year), the number of people on the organizing team (compared to last year), and the results from a post-event survey.

Speaking of surveys, I believe there's real value in asking people to answer a few questions from time to time. It can tell you whether your sense of how the ministry is going matches how other people are finding it. You can do this online, or you could hand out a printed questionnaire with some carefully worded questions or statements, asking people how much they agree with the statements on a scale of 1–10. For example:

> Thanks for bringing your children to Kids Church today. We'd love to get your feedback. Please tell us how much you agree with these statements on a scale of 1 (strongly disagree) to 10 (strongly agree).
>
> My child(ren) looks forward to coming to Kids Church each week.
>
> ① ② ③ ④ ⑤ ⑥ ⑦ ⑧ ⑨ ⑩
>
> The material and lessons at Kids Church help my child(ren) know and love Jesus.
>
> ① ② ③ ④ ⑤ ⑥ ⑦ ⑧ ⑨ ⑩
>
> The leaders know my child(ren) and try to suit the lessons to them.
>
> ① ② ③ ④ ⑤ ⑥ ⑦ ⑧ ⑨ ⑩
>
> How often do you read the Bible (or a children's Bible) with your child(ren)?
> *Every day – Every few days – Every week – Every few weeks – Every month – Less than every month*

Of course, the responses will not be completely accurate; it's just subjective data. And don't worry about which parent gave your team a two out of ten; choose to disassociate the names from the results. The average is the number that matters.

Six months later, you might hand out the same survey and compare the results. "It looks like children are looking forward to coming to Kids Church *more* now than they were six months ago. Great work, team! Why do you think that is?"

That's just one way you could do it. Maybe you and your team can think of another way that's a better fit for your situation. But whatever you choose to do, start with the conviction that it's worth keeping track of things because those things matter to God.

Reflection questions

1. How do you feel about tracking attendance and other measurable aspects of your ministry? What, if anything, makes you hesitant?

2. What numerical and measurable goals are relevant to your ministry? Do you and your team have a clear idea of the numerical goals you're aiming for together?

3. Are you already tracking anything? How is that happening? Could you add things to it? Could you delegate this role to someone on the team?

15

(RE)ASSIGN ROLES

One of the things a team leader will *often* do is deal with change. It might be a change in the team as someone takes a break or someone joins, or it might be a change in the people or program the team serves (such as when a new batch of young people arrives or a key family moves away). These are generally *reactive* changes—something outside the team leads to a change inside the team. And while it's important that we as team leaders help to oversee these reactive changes, we should also look to make *proactive* changes. Changing things— especially changing the roles and responsibilities that team members hold—helps your team rethink and re-pray the big prayer. It provides opportunities for growth and training. It prevents your team and its members from becoming stale and going through the motions. And it helps you step back and see ways to better run the program, or do the ministry, or love your team.

Pause for a moment and ask yourself two questions about your team: Who usually does what? And who put those people into those roles? Why are *they* doing *that*?

Many teams end up with unintentional role distribution: Bec always plans the food, Mitch always organizes the music, and James always leads the games. When this happens, team members can get set in their ways, or they can start identifying themselves by the job they do, rather than by the team they belong to. Even worse, they can become resistant to growth. When team members have worked out how to love a certain number of people, they can do that on repeat. But if the number of teenagers coming to the youth group doubled, the team members would have to change the way they do things. Growth means change, and most people don't really like change.

Change means growth

If growth means your team has to change, then is it completely unrealistic to say that changing your team roles might lead to growth? While it's certainly not a formula for growth, there is some correlation here. At the very least, when you invite your team to imagine change, it helps prepare them for growth because it lifts their eyes to the big prayer again. It helps the team stop and reconsider why they are doing things the way they are doing them, and if their current approach is really the best way to go. It enables them to rethink their own roles, and to revalue their teammates' roles.

So sometimes a team leader will say, "Hey team, I'd like us to change it up and keep things fresh. Next week, I'm going to get Angela and Bella to do X and Caleb and Doris to do Y. I think this will be a really helpful way for us to keep thinking about our big prayer and how we're all part of the team making it happen."

Changing things will almost certainly cause some initial frustration. Things will get missed, or jobs will be done poorly. Therefore, it's wise to limit how much change you introduce all at once. But the underlying principle is sound: changing things helps your team in the long run.

Same means growth

But you don't need to change roles to get the same effect. You can sit down with your team members and ask them about the roles they are doing. For example:

> Angela, you've been looking after the kids' registration process for a while now, right? How are you finding that? What things are going well, and what things do you think are worth changing?

> Chris, you've been part of the tech team for a few years now. I was wondering if we're under-utilizing you. Do you think we could get you training people so there are more people on the team in the future?

Ellie, you've been overseeing the youth group calendar for a while
now. I was wondering how you think it might change if we doubled
in size. Can we spend some time imagining that together? There
might be some ideas we come up with that we can implement now.

The aim here is to help your team members imagine changing the way they currently do their ministry. Invite them to break out of their habits and normal processes, and to consider if the way they're doing things is the best way. Essentially, this is just re-assigning the same role to people with a new job description. You're asking them to re-take the responsibility for the outcome, not just the task.

New teammates mean new team roles

The most obvious reason that you'll need to assign new roles to people is because you've recruited new team members. The new team member needs to fit into the team, and that means the other team members will need to shuffle around to fit them in. The most common way this works is that the new team member takes on a little bit of everyone's responsibilities—usually the jobs that nobody else likes doing! But that's not really the best way to share roles.

Another way to integrate a new team member is to completely re-jig the team structure. But this often leads to more pain because everyone must learn a new role at the same time (possibly while watching a teammate do their old role poorly).

There's no ideal way to bring on a new team member. It all depends on the team and the various roles people already do. You could get the new team member to shadow an existing member for a while and then take over that role, as the existing member takes on something new. You could ask the new team member to take on some of your responsibilities that you haven't delegated yet. Or you could ask your team how best to use a new team member and have a type-2 conversation together.

Rethink role descriptions

This might be controversial, but I avoid written role descriptions for individual team members. Instead, I want to keep focusing on why the team exists, and from there I want to keep inviting individual team members to be prepared to do whatever role helps the team towards that big purpose. Roles come and go in the moment, but the team's big purpose remains fairly steady. If you give someone a written role description, it lasts only as long as the role remains the same, and the role only remains the same if your ministry doesn't grow or change. But ministry is always about people, and people grow and change. Show me a well-written role description, and within three months I'll show you a scrap of paper that doesn't really help anyone.

But won't your team members feel overburdened if they don't have clear, written role descriptions? Could someone feel like a failure because they missed something they didn't realize was their job?

If a team member misses something because they didn't realize it was their job, that's probably your responsibility as team leader. You might not have had enough conversations with them to make sure they grasped that one thing. You might have assumed they understood or that they would remember (I regularly suggest my team members write things down rather than trying to keep them in their heads). Could you write it down for them? Sure. But if you do, be aware that your written notes carry more weight than their own written notes. So, make sure it's understood as a *temporary* role description. Make sure your team know that roles change with people and with growth. They're not responsible for doing the role; they're responsible for being part of the team.

Move people up the why-how spectrum

When I talk about re-assigning roles, I don't mean that you just reshuffle the deck at random; it's more than just swapping people's responsibilities for the sake of it. The ultimate goal is to move your team further up the why-how spectrum that we first saw back in chapter 7:

← Principles   *Practicals →*

Team's big prayer	Team's gospel culture	Program values and standards	Desired program outcomes	Who does what	When things are due	How things are done

Many teams operate with the leader doing almost everything on this spectrum. The leader sets the big prayer, cares about the team culture, upholds the values and standards, describes the outcomes the team is working towards, decides which team member does each role, tells people when things are due, and tops it all off by spending a fair amount of time telling people how to do things.

But what if we swapped this around so the team took responsibility for most of the boxes in the why-how spectrum? Imagine a team where the members cared about the culture being Christian, where they had input into and refined the program's values and standards, where they helped each other understand the outcomes they were seeking, where they decided who did what, and where they set their own deadlines and worked out how best to get things done.

These two teams—one where the leader does almost everything, and one where the team members take much more responsibility—might do the same ministry activity, and they might look the same from the outside. But the experience of being part of these two teams will be very different. In the first team, members just do what they're told. In the second team, every member feels responsible for the team and for its ministry. We're aiming for this second type of team.

That might seem like a fantasy when you think about your current team members. That's okay, because every team has to start somewhere. The key is to start sharing aspects of the responsibility you already feel as the leader. This means delegating some of the 'higher-level' responsibilities to your team members, so they have authority to make real decisions that can improve how the team functions and how it loves people.

I'd love to say this is easy, but my own experience has shown me that team leaders often find it hard to even imagine what this might look like. I can get stuck in a mindset that assumes no-one else can do the various jobs that I'm doing. At this point, I'm the bottleneck stopping team members from taking on higher responsibilities. Personally, I've found the best solution to get out of this rut has been to ask another leader to help me think about my team and who does what. As I tell them all the things I do, they might interrupt and ask: "Is there any reason you can't ask one of your team members to do that job for you?" I'll usually respond with something like, "Oh my goodness, why didn't I think of that before?"

In other words, as you (re)assign roles within the team, keep in mind many of your current leadership roles might need to be assigned to others. And that's good for them, good for you, and good for the team.

Reflection questions

1. Are you happy with the division of responsibilities among your team members? If you could build the team again (with the same people), how would you divide up the roles differently?

2. Imagine if your ministry team had to love twice as many people as it does now. How would it need to change? What would the team need to look like, and how would your role look different?

3. If you had a new and excited team member offer themselves to your team tomorrow, what would be the first role you'd want them to fill, and why? Which of your team members would it affect the most (other than yourself)?

16

PLAY ON THE TEAM

Throughout most of this book, I've been encouraging you to be the coach on the sidelines—to watch, think and communicate. My focus has been on the conversations and discussions you have with your team members to help them get their ministry done. It could give the impression that you never get your hands dirty.

But the reality is that you will 'do ministry' with your team. In fact, it's my personal experience that I get to do some of my most enjoyable pastoral ministry as the leader of the team.

Leading is ministry

First, it's important to remember that leading your team *is* ministry. You aren't just facilitating others to do the real ministry; you're doing real ministry yourself. Consider how Paul says Christ "gave ... pastors and teachers to equip the saints for the work of ministry" (Eph 4:11–12). A key aspect of pastoral ministry is helping others to do ministry. You're serving Jesus by helping your team serve Jesus. You're encouraging them to pray, forgive one another and repent. You're opening the Bible with them, and you care about their lives. Don't diminish the real pastoral value of being a team leader as though it's just 'people management'. We don't *manage* the Christians on our teams; we *love* them and *serve* them by helping them serve Jesus. That means when you have that little chat with Harry to encourage him while a ministry event is in progress, you're doing ministry. When you give Jenny some feedback about her talk, you're doing ministry. When you pray for your team members through the week, you're doing ministry.

Ministry as an informal participant

Second, when you delegate responsibilities and tasks to your team members, you have a wonderful opportunity to observe your ministry program as a participant. You can sit shoulder to shoulder with the people your team is trying to love, and you can have good conversations with them. I still remember the first time I was able to sit in the church I serve as pastor, having delegated everything from the setup to the sermon. It was wonderful—not because I didn't have to do anything, but because I could talk to the very people the church was serving. I didn't stop doing ministry; I was freed up to oversee the ministry and participate with others in church.

One of the best ways to oversee your team is by sitting with the very people your team is trying to love, experiencing the ministry from their perspective.

Joining in with the team

But there will also be times when you jump in and serve side-by-side with your team members. Even though team leadership is primarily about being the coach on the sideline, there will be moments when we need to get up off the bleachers and run onto the field with the team.

It's worth thinking about why we might need to join the team in this way.

It could be that someone is sick, and you need to step in to fill a hole on the team that day. There might be more people in attendance than expected, and your team needs a hand to get everything done for that many people. Or you might just have been unable to secure the number of team members you wanted for an event. These are all fair reasons for a team leader to strap on their boots and run onto the field.

The only issue is when this becomes too regular: you enjoy it, your team members get a kick out of it, and things will almost certainly run well that week (because you're probably better at some of the jobs than they are). Don't get addicted to doing this! Stepping into these roles should be clearly talked about as a one-time or short-term thing. If you keep finding yourself *in the team*, you'll very quickly lose your capacity to care about everything you're meant to be doing *for the team.*

Not more equal than others

Another reason you might join in on the team is to demonstrate that you're not 'above' your team members. This might be a uniquely Australian concern, but since we have an issue with tall poppies,[38] it is helpful to remind our team (and ourselves) that we're not better than them, and we don't turn up our nose at 'hard work'. It's just that the hard work we do as team leaders is often unseen by our team members. Therefore, there's value in showing that you're still just like them.

When I was a teenager, one of my soccer coaches would gather us at half-time and grumble out some frustrated choice words—but then he'd pick up the discarded orange peels and walk them to the nearest bin. He was definitely *the boss*, but it wasn't beneath him to do a disgusting job. Similarly, as the team leader you might regularly volunteer to take out the trash, clean the toilets, or help with the pack-up. Whatever it might be, don't use "I'm the leader" as an excuse to turn up your nose at something that needs to be done.

38 'Tall-poppy syndrome' is a common expression in Australia. It refers to the typically Australian habit of critiquing people who appear successful or hold authority. The critique is often done through being disrespectful or dismissive when people above us lean into their authority or success.

Reflection questions

1. How do you feel about the idea that simply leading your team *is* ministry—just different from the ministry they are doing?

2. How often do you step into the breach and act as a team member alongside your team? Has this become a habit, or is it irregular?

3. How will you show that menial jobs aren't beneath you as the leader? What's something you can do that's small but significant?

PART 5

TOOLS TO HELP YOU LEAD

Congratulations! Assuming you haven't just flipped to this page, you've worked through a lot of material and wrestled with many important aspects of being a team leader. There's a lot to think about, right? As you'll have seen, central to the task is *having conversations*. But it's not just any conversations; it's about having the right type of conversation—the conversation your team needs you to have with them in the moment.

But is that it? Is team leading simply about how you communicate with your team members in the moment?

Essentially, yes.

As a team leader, you are meant to shape your team members. You should help them to think along the same lines as you and make the kinds of decisions you'd want them to make. There's really no way to do that other than communicating *a lot*. More than anything else, team leading means talking—lots and lots of talking. That's why I've shaped so much of this book around the four conversations tool.

Yet team leading cannot be entirely reduced to talking. It also involves *thinking*. It's about *considering*, and only then communicating. It's *assessing* and then articulating. So, while the four conversations tool helps us work out how to do the talking, communicating and articulating, what about the thinking, considering and assessing?

That's what the tools in this final section of the book will help you to do.

17

KNOW YOURSELF
(AND YOUR TEAM) BETTER

Many life experiences reveal more about ourselves than we expect. Whether it's living in a different culture, becoming a parent, or changing churches, we often look back and think, "I never realized this about myself until I went through ..." The same is true of being a team leader. I'm always finding out more about myself as I lead teams—usually things I wish I'd known earlier. That's why it's helpful for you as a team leader to use tools to understand yourself better. You can also use these tools to help your team members understand themselves, which in turn helps you to understand them.

One of my favourite tools is the 'working genius' model, created by management expert Patrick Lencioni.

The six types of working genius (workinggenius.com)

The basic idea of this tool is that there are six types of 'work' that people bring to a team: Wonder, Invention, Discernment, Galvanizing, Enablement and Tenacity (offering the acronym 'WIDGET'). Lencioni suggests that most people only *enjoy* doing two of these, they can *manage* another two, and they probably get *exhausted* or *frustrated* doing the other two. Every person has a different pair that they find *enjoyable*, *manageable* and *frustrating*.

Below is a summary of these six types, but I'm going to rephrase aspects of the model to make it more applicable for Christian ministry teams.[39]

The gift of Wonder

This is the person who loves asking "why?" and saying "I wonder ..." They're hesitant to jump into new things, and prefer to mull over the potential causes and reasons behind what's happening. If they're in a band, they ask, "Why are we doing this song?" If they're helping with children, they ask, "I wonder if the kids are really getting this, or if the parents are on board". These people ask the questions that spark new ideas.

The gift of Invention

These people love coming up with ideas and saying, "How about we try this?" They are quick to offer solutions and ways to make things happen better. This is the welcoming team member who wants to try changing where things go every second week, or the study-group leader who comes up with a last-minute change they think will work better. These people are quick to see new ways to solve problems.

The gift of Discernment

These people are great at bringing their wisdom to bear on an idea. They might not be the one asking the big question (that's the gift of Wonder) or coming up with the solution (the gift of Invention), but they know it when they see it. They have a knack of seeing how things will work together, or knowing if others will get on board with an idea. This is the evangelism team member who hears the idea and says, "Yes! I can see that working well for this reason, and for that reason". They also help shut down ideas that won't work for the team.

The gift of Galvanizing

These are the people who love getting other people together. Whether they're big and loud or softly spoken, these are the people who other people notice and follow. When they say, "Let's do it!" other people say, "I'm in!" This is that one

---

39 You'll find the full assessment tool plus a range of related resources at workinggenius.com. If you're interested in purchasing and completing the full assessment, it would be worth reading the 'Rollout guide for Working Genius in churches' found at workinggenius.com/resources.

family who says they're going to the church picnic, which means everyone else will go too. This is the band leader who people find it easy to follow, or the children's teacher who all the kids gravitate towards. These people just have a gift for getting other people on board.

The gift of Enablement

These are the people who love helping others. They get excited by an idea, and they love getting it off the ground and making it work. They are quick to offer help, they're the first to say they can join in, and they'll often try new things because they see it would be helpful. These are the welcome-team members who say, "I've done my bit; what's next?" Or they'll come with a list of names of people who need to get followed up because you mentioned it as a passing idea at the last meeting.

The gift of Tenacity

These people love ticking boxes on their to-do list. They get a sense of joy and fulfilment from seeing things through to the end and doing what had been decided. What they might lack in spontaneity, they make up for in faithfulness to the task. These are the study-group leaders who don't miss a week, or the welcome-team members who chase up every last person. These people love to help you keep your team organized.

As you probably know, there are plenty of other assessment tools on the market—such as CliftonStrengths (formerly Strengths Finder) or the Myers-Briggs personality test. Whatever tool you use—or if you prefer an informal process of reflection—knowing the types of gifts each of your team members brings helps you to give them roles they'll love, and to be more understanding when they struggle to do things they find hard. It also helps to understand your own tendencies and how it might affect those in your team.

Let me tell you how it played out with Steve.

Steve and I had been looking at the six types of Working Genius to help him think about his team. He had identified himself as high on Enablement, and low on Invention. We were planning to talk through the rest of his team, but we both had to get to another meeting where a bunch of team leaders were going to discuss a big issue hanging over our heads: our church was moving. We had outgrown the small school hall and classrooms we were using, and we were planning to start meeting in another building.

As Steve and I looked around the room, we saw the various other team leaders. Steve looked at me with a raised eyebrow and said, "Hey, do you reckon we can spot what Working Genius type everyone is?"

"Sounds fun", I replied. I took out the sheet we had been working through with the six types and their descriptions, and put it on the table where we could both see it.

John kicked off the meeting. "So, in a few weeks we're going to be at the new venue. What do you think we need to discuss as a team?"

Emily jumped in: "I was thinking this might be a great opportunity to re-imagine what a church can be like from the ground up. I mean, what does it really mean to be a church anyway?"

That got Olivia excited: "Yeah, we could have dramatic readings, and meals after church, and the kids can arrive early and play games. Maybe we can reach out to see if there are any local clubs who might want to partner with us and run some events in the holidays!"

William seemed concerned. "I'm not sure we should just jump into anything. There's probably a bunch of other churches who have had to go through the same thing, and we could learn a lot from them."

I glanced at Steve and nodded towards the page in front of us.

Steve took out a pen and next to Wonder wrote: "Emily for sure".

Then beside Invention, he wrote: "Olivia?"

Then pointed to Discernment and scribbled, "William?"

I couldn't help chuckle; he was spot on. Emily loved thinking about the 'what if?' and the 'why?' but she struggled to see the whole picture. Olivia could come up with ideas as easily as she could breathe, but she didn't have William's discernment; he was a natural sceptic who only seemed to feel comfortable with a plan that was already tried and tested.

John tried to get everyone back on track and the meeting went on. A question came up about whether everyone at church knew about the plans. Amanda jumped in: "Well, I've already spoken to a few people; the Taylors and the Wilsons are all over it, and I messaged the Andersons last week and they said they were going to talk to the Harris brothers and their mum. And I'm planning to chat with a few others this week."

Steve smiled and pointed to the page where it said Galvanizer and marked it with a big tick.

A bit later, James spoke up: "Are there things we need to move from the school to the new place? I'm happy to organize a truck."

Steve jumped on James' offer: "There are a few tubs of Kids Church gear we need moved. If you moved them, that would really *enable* me to get the kids' team ready."

I smiled and gave Steve a nod.

Nat hadn't spoken yet, and looked around the table. "Is anyone taking notes? Maybe I'll do that so we can make sure we get everything done."

Quick as a flash, Steve put a tick next to Tenacity and whispered under his breath, "Bingo!"

One of the values of these six categories is that they help explain why some people find other people frustrating. Someone who loves Wonder and someone who loves Tenacity will run a team meeting in very different ways, usually to the utter frustration of the other. But remember, there's nothing spiritual about these types or categories. And it is important not to box people too quickly or too rigidly with one and not the other. They're just a helpful tool for us as team leaders to understand ourselves and our team members better. And, by God's grace, they're tools that might also help us to love them and lead them better.

Reflection questions

1. Look through the six 'Working Genius' gifts. Which two do you think you naturally enjoy? Which two do you think you find frustrating?

- wonder
- invention
- discernment
- galvanizing
- enablement
- tenacity

2. What about your team members? Write out your team members' names, and try to put a type next to each name. Are your team members like you, or are they different? Are their styles and gifts mainly the same as one another, or are they quite varied?

3. How might a range of gifts and preferences help your team to function well?

18

CONSIDER WHAT SEASON YOUR TEAM IS IN

Even in the ministry world, your team will go through phases, or seasons. One way to think about these normal team phases is to split the life of a team into four stages: Forming, Storming, Norming and Performing.[40] These phases seem to be a normal part of team life, so it's worth considering where your team might find itself now, and where it might be going.

Let's think about what characterizes each of the four seasons.

Forming

In the Forming phase, the team is just starting out, or a large portion of the team is new. Team members are trying to work out their roles—not just regarding the ministry, but also in relation to one another and to you. They're all trying to work out the unspoken social rules and the culture of the team.

Most teams in the Forming stage will get some things right, but they will do so inefficiently. For example, a welcoming team might get everything set up amazingly well on a Sunday, but it might have taken twice as long as it should have because people are re-doing each other's jobs, while other things slip between the cracks.

40 BW Tuckman, 'Developmental sequence in small groups', *Psychological Bulletin*, 1965, 63 (6):384–399.

The Forming stage is the establishing stage; your team is figuring out what type of team they are going to be. And since everything's new, people normally have a lot of grace and understanding. They won't get things right, but they also won't get overly annoyed at each other.

Storming

The Storming phase refers to a difficult stage in the life of the team: "things are getting a bit stormy". It usually happens straight after the team feels like they're getting the hang of things and people start holding each other to a higher standard—that's when things start to fall apart. Perhaps the members of the welcoming team start to challenge and frustrate each other: Bob gets annoyed at the way Peter does things, and Peter gets annoyed that Bob's butting in. The relationships get 'stormy' as things don't work smoothly. This can also be when tensions arise and team members want you to step in and tell someone on the team to change. In fact, any changes to the team or the ministry can generate some 'storminess' in the team.

The trick with the Storming phase is to keep discussions in type 2 or type 3. Don't try to solve your team's issues by stepping in as an authoritarian figure, but don't leave them to resolve their issues on their own. As the team leader, your role is to encourage your team to talk with each other, share ideas, work through their difficulties, and agree on values and principles. When these conflicts get sorted out, that's when your team hits the next phase ...

Norming

The Norming phase is when things start falling into place and your team starts working well together. They start to get over their frustrations, and they figure out how to work together. Bob will tell Peter, "Hey, how about you just look after the Connect table, and I'll look after the coffee? Maybe that will be easier."

This is when team members start to better understand their place in the team and their role in the overall ministry. You play an important role in encouraging them to keep making thoughtful decisions and to keep each other in the loop. They start to feel like a team, and they support each other.

But as good as this sounds, this isn't the last phase.

Performing

The Performing phase is when a team starts improving things by itself or managing change extremely well. In ministry terms, this is when Bob says to Peter, "Hey, the Connect table is working really well. Do you have any suggestions for the coffee stuff I'm doing? Can we work better together somehow?" Or it might mean the welcoming team reorganizes itself to improve efficiency, or they come to you and say, "We think we need to put on a meal one week to help people feel part of the community. We've picked a date, and we have some ideas about what to do. Did you want us to go ahead, or talk about it some more?"

The Performing stage is lots of fun, but it usually takes a long time to get there. And every time you add a new team member, or the ministry needs to change to manage growth, you go through a little cycle of Forming, Storming, Norming and Performing all over again. Yay.

Understanding that teams go through seasons helps us to remember the importance of focusing on the three things team leaders *always* do. No matter what season your team is in, the best thing we can do for them is lead them in prayer about the big purpose of the team, cultivate a gospel-shaped culture, and keep talking about the values and principles behind everything the team does.

No matter the season, watch and communicate. Think and speak. That's what team leaders do.

Reflection questions

1. Why are these stages of team life helpful to keep in mind?

2. What stage do you think your team is in right now?

3. Is there anything (or anyone) holding your team back from getting through this current season and moving towards Performing?

19

ASSESS YOUR TEAM'S PERFORMANCE

Another helpful framework for thinking about your team is the acronym PERFORM.[41] This describes what you're aiming at as a high-performing team. What follows is a very quick summary, modified to fit a Christian mindset:

P: Purposeful
E: Equipped
R: Relational
F: Fun
O: Organized
R: Reflective
M: Motivated by the gospel

Let's briefly consider each one.

---

41   See K Blanchard, D Carew and E Panisi-Carew, *The One Minute Manager Builds High Performing Teams*, Thorsons, 2017, p 11. Their original acronym is: Purpose and Values, Empowerment, Relationships and Communication, Flexibility, Optimal Performance, Recognition and Appreciation, and Morale.

Purposeful

A great team has a clear gospel purpose. They know why they exist (for the church and for Jesus). They understand the big prayer. Every team member can express this in their own words. But more than that, they *believe* it. They're excited about it.

Can each of your team members express the purpose of the team in their own words?

And more than just repeating it, do they believe it? Is it important to them? Are they convicted about it?

 THE TEAM LEADER'S HANDBOOK

Equipped

Great team members don't just understand their responsibilities; they also know how to do them, and to do them well. They have the tools and the skills to get their jobs done, and they know how to ask for help if they need it.

Does your team have the skills and understanding to do their jobs without you by their side?

Are there jobs that keep coming back to you?

What are the jobs that only one or two team members can do? How can you get them to teach others?

Relational

A great team trusts one another, cares for one another, and loves one another. Your team members are not just 'human resources'—they're Jesus' people who show the fruit of the Spirit towards each other. A performing team will treat each other with the respect and kindness appropriate for those who call on Jesus as their Lord.

Does your team care about each other? Are they interested in each other's lives? Are they quick to forgive, or are they quick to get frustrated? Do they pray for each other?

Fun

This takes the previous point one step further. Great teams have fun together. They can relax and joke when the time's right. Get your team to eat together and play games together, and have each other over at your houses. Fun is both a *cause* and a *result* of teams growing in trust. That is, a high performing team isn't just relational; they go one step further and enjoy each other's company.

Does your team have a bit of a laugh together, or is it all serious all the time?

Are there people who bring down the vibe of the team? Are you ever that person?

Organized

Great teams have systems, lists and plans that they stick to. In fact, it's not just that they have a plan; it's that they have confidence in one another that the agreed plans will happen. They can trust one another so that when one person says something will happen, everyone knows that's that. Being organized also means reminding each other and keeping each other in the loop.

Does your team have a clear plan that people can find easily and follow with confidence?

Does your team trust one another? Are the individual members reliable?

How easy is it to find out who's responsible for what on the team?

Reflective

Great teams are good at self-reflection and learning from what went well and what didn't go well. They can handle a bit of criticism, and they feel comfortable raising concerns with each other about how the team (and the team leader) is going. But it's not just negative—great teams are quick to praise each other when they see one another doing great things.

Is your team open about how they think they're going? Do they congratulate each other and cheer each other on? How interested are they in improving together?

Motivated by the gospel

This last point is the most important of all: our teams are nothing if they are not gospel-centred, motivated by a desire to glorify God and grow his kingdom in love. As Paul says, "if I give all my possessions and I give all my body so I may boast, but do it without love, I'm nothing" (1 Cor 13:3).

Great ministry teams love serving Jesus and his church. They overflow with thankfulness to God. They have hearts full of praise for Jesus and lips dripping with prayers. They are grounded in God's word, and they want to please their Lord through the team working well together and serving others. They can see the connection between Jesus' gospel and the work they are doing, and it is this connection that excites them and fuels all that they do together.

Do your team members love Jesus? Are they serving him as they serve in your team? Are they passionate about seeing the gospel grow and bear fruit through the team?

How do they pray about the team and their roles? Are they thankful and grateful?

These seven ideas provide a series of lenses through which you can look at your team and consider where you might need to put some renewed effort. (For example, we've found many volunteer-led teams at our church have tended towards an overbearing sense of formality and strictness. They forget to have fun together, usually because the team leader feels so much pressure to have a high-performing team!)

But remember, as a team leader your job is to help your team members take responsibility for the team too. Maybe ask them how they think they're going, and get them to suggest ways to help the team PERFORM at a higher level, for God's glory.

Reflection questions

1. Which of the PERFORM points is your team going well in and which one are they struggling with? Which category do you see as your team's strongest? Which one is the weakest?

2. As the team leader, how are you going to encourage the aspect they are already doing well in? What can you do to celebrate it? How can you help them to grow in the area(s) where they are currently weakest?

3. Ask God to help you shape and guide your team for the sake of others and for the growth of the gospel.

LET'S GO!

My big prayer in writing this book has always been that God would use these ideas to help you love your team members so that you can joyfully and fruitfully serve Jesus together and play your part in the growth of his gospel. I firmly believe that if our churches were filled with team leaders who deeply loved their team members and were equipped with the skills to serve their teams well, it would make an enormous difference. The thought of seeing thousands of volunteers help other volunteers to undertake some great gospel endeavours is truly awesome. I hope and pray this book might help you lead others to do great things for the kingdom.

But I want to come back to one key idea that I raised right near the start of the book.

The mind shift from team member to team leader is massive. It took me a long time to learn it, and I still see myself falling back into old habits. I watch my team run out on the field, and I can't help but jump the fence and run out there too. I'm a chronic player-coach.

But I believe my team needs me to be their coach. I'm convinced the most loving thing I can be is a support, a guide, a trainer and a leader. That will make them a better crew. That will have the biggest gospel footprint in years to come. That's the Christian impact I pray I'll be able to leave.

So, I hope you'll join me in continuing to grow as a Christian team leader. I hope your team members will feel supported and responsible for what they're doing. I hope you'll be calling your team members to step up and take on team leadership roles themselves. (Maybe you could buy them their own copy of this book.)

Above all, I hope the gospel continues to grow through Jesus' people working together for his glory.

Feedback on this resource

We really appreciate getting feedback about our resources—not just suggestions for how to improve them, but also positive feedback and ways they can be used. We especially love to hear that the resources may have helped someone in their Christian growth.

You can send feedback to us via the 'Feedback' menu in our online store, or write to us at info@matthiasmedia.com.au.

WITH THANKS

While the metanarrative account of my conversations with Steve are largely fictional, Steve is a real guy who I had the privilege of training while he did a ministry apprenticeship. The conversations recorded in this book were mainly derived from real conversations I had with him and with my other ministry apprentices: Ben, Nick, Kiwi, Andy and Nathan. I have learned most of my lessons from the mistakes we made together. Thank you, brothers, for your patience (and forgiveness) and for the joy of serving Jesus together like a father with his sons!

I also want to give special acknowledgement to Greg Lee, my trainer when I did a ministry apprenticeship, and my pastor and boss since then. Greg, I doubt I'd understand type-4 conversations as well as I do without having experienced them from you regularly. The same goes for the awesome staff and members of Hunter Bible Church. Thanks for letting me watch, discuss, argue and learn with you as brothers and sisters in Christ.

A huge thanks to Scott Parry-Jones for introducing me to the four conversations model. You've been an amazing blessing, brother.

But what I really want to say is thanks to Julie. xxoo

☸ matthiasmedia

Matthias Media is an evangelical publishing ministry that seeks to persuade all Christians of the truth of God's purposes in Jesus Christ as revealed in the Bible, and equip them with high-quality resources, so that by the work of the Holy Spirit they will:

- abandon their lives to the honour and service of Christ in daily holiness and decision-making
- pray constantly in Christ's name for the fruitfulness and growth of his gospel
- speak the Bible's life-changing word whenever and however they can— in the home, in the world and in the fellowship of his people.

Our wide range of resources includes Bible studies, books, training courses, tracts and children's material. To find out more, and to access samples and free downloads, visit our website:

matthiasmedia.com

How to buy our resources

1. Direct from us over the internet:
   - in the US: matthiasmedia.com
   - in Australia: matthiasmedia.com.au

2. Direct from us by phone: please visit our website for current phone contact information.

3. Through a range of outlets in various parts of the world. Visit **matthiasmedia.com/contact** for details about recommended retailers in your part of the world.

4. Trade enquiries can be addressed to:
   - in the US and Canada: sales@matthiasmedia.com
   - in Australia and the rest of the world: sales@matthiasmedia.com.au

Growth Groups

By Colin Marshall

This practical ten-week training program develops effective small group leaders, but it is also useful for all Christian ministry, because it deals with the fundamentals of gospel work. It trains leaders to teach the Bible and pray with other Christians, to answer questions, to grow individuals, to gather together fellow-believers in evangelistic enterprise. In short, this book by Colin Marshall will equip leaders to grow Christians and grow the gospel. This manual can also stand alone as a valuable guide for leaders to work through on their own if they can't join a course with other leaders.

For more information or to order contact:

Matthias Media
sales@matthiasmedia.com.au
matthiasmedia.com.au

Matthias Media (USA)
sales@matthiasmedia.com
matthiasmedia.com

Growth and Change

By Andrew Heard with Geoff Robson

"I honestly believe this could prove to be one of the most important books (after the Bible, of course) for church leaders in our time."
—Richard Coekin

"How can we care about growing a church and not lose our theological moorings in the process? Andrew Heard shows us the way."
—Ed Stetzer

"Andrew Heard is well known and well trusted in Australia, his homeland. Now we pray that his influence may multiply exponentially around the world."
—D.A. Carson

"A stirring call to radically rethink our trellises for the sake of growing the vine."—Tony Payne

"Every leader of a church or Christian organization should read this."
—Robert S. Kinney

For more information or to order contact:

Matthias Media
sales@matthiasmedia.com.au
matthiasmedia.com.au

Matthias Media (USA)
sales@matthiasmedia.com
matthiasmedia.com

The Trellis and the Vine

By Colin Marshall and Tony Payne

There is vine work: the prayerful preaching and teaching of the word of God to see people converted and grow to maturity as disciples of Christ. Vine work is the Great Commission.

And there is trellis work: creating and maintaining the physical and organisational structures and programs that support vine work and its growth.

What's the state of the trellis and the vine in your part of the world? Has trellis work taken over, as it has a habit of doing? Is the vine work being done by very few (perhaps only the pastor and only on Sundays)? And is the vine starting to wilt as a result?

In *The Trellis and the Vine*, Colin Marshall and Tony Payne dig into the Bible's view of Christian ministry. They find that a major mind-shift is required if we are to fulfil the Great Commission of Christ and see the vine flourish again.

For more information or to order contact:

Matthias Media
sales@matthiasmedia.com.au
matthiasmedia.com.au

Matthias Media (USA)
sales@matthiasmedia.com
matthiasmedia.com

AVAILABLE ONLINE

The Vine Project

By Colin Marshall and Tony Payne

The Trellis and the Vine proposed a "ministry mind-shift that changes everything". *The Vine Project* shows how that mind-shift can and must shape every aspect of what you are doing as a congregation of Christ's people to make disciples of all nations.

If you found *The Trellis and the Vine* compelling, this book provides a roadmap and resources for the church-wide culture change you want to see. It will guide your ministry leadership team through a five-phase process for growth and change, with biblical input, practical ideas, resources, case studies, exercises and projects along the way.

For more information or to order contact:

Matthias Media
sales@matthiasmedia.com.au
matthiasmedia.com.au

Matthias Media (USA)
sales@matthiasmedia.com
matthiasmedia.com